THE HISTORY OF HOOE BARTON FARM

FROM DOMESDAY TO 200

ROBIN BLYTHE-LORD NDD ATD ADAE

Hooe Barton Barn and Farmhouse in 1968
Photograph: Stanley Goodman. Collection of Sheila Coleman

©Robin Blythe-Lord. 2001

First edition. October 2001

All rights reserved. No part of this publication may be reproduced, stored in a retrieval system or transmitted in any form or by any means without the prior permission of the copyright holder.

Published by The Friends of Hooe Barn.
Camelot, Amacre Drive, Hooe, Plymouth PL9 9RJ
Tel: Chairman: 01752 402746 Publicity: 01752 403321

Printed by Blackfriars Contract Division. 01752 220451

ISBN 0-9541562-0-X

Acknowledgements

Bibliography

Many thanks to everyone who took the time to talk, advise and loan material.

Esther Arnold
Maureen Attrill, Plymouth City Art Gallery
Pat and Bryan Barber
Zoë Bibby, Proofreader
Lesley Blythe-Lord
Chris Burlace, Historic Caravan Club
Eric Burridge
Sheila Coleman
Roger Dean, PCC
John Emery
Doreen Glinn
Terry Guswell
Cynthia Gwilliam
Barbara Jennings
Trevor Johns, PCC
Roy Hopper
Ivy Langdon
William and Di MacMonagle
Ian Maxted, Devon Libraries, Exeter
Christine North, County Archivist, Cornwall
The Old Plymouth Society
Mary Outhwaite
Jean Parsons
Joan Phillips
Shirley Pippin, Historic Caravan Club
Plymouth and West Devon Record Office Staff
Plymouth Library Staff
Eddie Rendle
Herbert Rendell
Chris Robinson
Alf Salmon
John Symons
Mary Skilton
Peter Scott, PCC
Frances Tapley
Mr and Mrs Thorn
Richard Tidmarsh, PCC
Jacqueline Truscott
Raymond Westlake
Roger Westlake
Western Morning News, Evening Herald
June Whyte
Dennis Wilkinson, Plymouth University
Brian Willdern

Clamp, Arthur. 'Hooe and Turnchapel Remembered.' 1981. Self Published.

Devon Constabulary.
Air Raid Damage Reports 1941-45.

Firth, Anthony. Watson, Kit & Ellis, Chris. 'Tamar Estuaries Historic Environment'. 1998. Plymouth Archaeology. ISBN 1-85522-592-1

Gardiner, Julie. (Ed). 'Resurgam!' 2000. Wessex Archaeology. ISBN 1-874350-33-7

Gill, Crispin. 'Plymouth, A New History'. 1993. Devon Books. ISBN 0-86114-882-7.

Gill, Crispin. 'Plymouth River'. 1997. Devon Books. ISBN 0-86114-911-4.

Hinde, Thomas. (Ed) 'The Domesday Book, England's heritage then and now. 1985. Phoebe Phillips Editions.

Hudd, Roy. 'Cavalcade of Variety Acts'. 1998. Robson Books Ltd. ISBN 1-86105-20-65

Tidmarsh, Richard. 'Hooe Barn, an Evaluation.' 1995. Internal paper, Plymouth City Council.

Langdon, Ivy. 'The Plymstock Connection'. 1995. Westcountry Books. ISBN 1-898386-14-5.

Pye, Andrew and Woodward, Freddy. 'The Historic Defences of Plymouth'. 1996. Cornwall County Council. ISBN 1-898166-46-3.

*All photographs by Robin Blythe-Lord
unless otherwise stated.*

This book is dedicated to the memory of the late Stanley Goodman, secretary of the Old Plymouth Society, through whose efforts the Barn was saved from demolition. Photo collection of Esther Arnold.

CONTENTS

Hay Cutting circa 1800

Hooe Lake, the Cattewater and Laira. 2001. Taken from the top of the Brakes immediately behind the Barn which is slightly hidden by the trees in the centre of the picture

FORWORD

At school I suffered history. It was 'taught' in the most boring, uninteresting and appalling way imaginable. The teacher would enter the classroom and say:

"Copy out pages 34 to 54 from your History textbook. What you haven't done during this lesson complete for homework."

History was lists, abstract dates, dead people, meaningless treaties, unfathomable wheeler dealings, wars won and lost, acts of parliament invoked and repealed, strategies planned and reams and reams of notes to be memorised. Outside the sun shone, the traffic moved, you could smell the new mown grass, Bill Haley was rockin' and History stood no chance. For some reason this particular teacher was not sacked for crimes against humanity. Had our luck been in he would have been hung by the toenails if we had met him on a dark night, but our luck had gone for a coffee at El Sombrero.

This went on for a long long time, at least a year, maybe more. We were being prepared for GCE 'O' levels. I learned to write quickly and legibly and to copy accurately; I learned rote facts without understanding. I learned nothing of it except dislike. I passed History, so that was allright. Then I dropped it like a dead rat.

It took me many years to realise that History was about people. People like you, me and that shifty looking person over there. People who were ambitious, heroic, stupid, brilliant, corrupt, venal, self seeking, altruistic, devious, philanthropic, criminal, traitorous, vicious, hopeless, wonderful... Once I understood that these people were so like us, that they were trying to live as best they could with the facilities at their disposal, I realised that History was interesting. These people had shaped the world I lived in; they had sculpted the landscape, given rise to the problems, provided the freedoms and already invented the wheel. They were responsible for *now*!

You and I live in a bubble of time bounded by our lifetime. Easy to think that all we see and do is unique. Natural human vanity? Possibly.

"Well, that might not have worked before but things are different now!"

However the 'things' are mostly technological facilitators such as Transport, Communications and Technology. You and I are as ambitious, heroic, stupid, brilliant, corrupt, venal, self seeking, altruistic, devious, philanthropic, criminal, traitorous, vicious, hopeless and wonderful as our ancestors. We just have different tools with which to pursue our aims and we seem to have learned little from our past.

In this history of Hooe Barton Farm I have included the conversations with people because their memories and stories have been so very fascinating and personal. Snapshots of a past but similar life. You may find there is a bit more humanity than is usual for a 'history book' but hey, that's life, or in this case, History.

Robin Blythe-Lord

NOTES

Names change over the years. Hooe Barton Farm has, variously, been known as Hooe Manor, West Hooe Farm, Hooe Barton Farm, Hooe Manor Farm at Westhoobury and just Hooe Farm as well as by the name of every owner and farmer who ran it; latterly it was Bayly's, Hine's, then Sherrell's, then Ford's even though at the time of the Hine's it was owned by the Bayly's and while the Fords ran it it was owned by the Sherrell's.

For the purposes of clarity and consistency it is referred to here as Hooe Barton Farm.

The name Barton is derived from Barley Tonne, a place where barley was stored and a direct reference to the large barn. A farm was only deemed worthy of including the title 'Barton' in its name if it was larger than 300 acres. The name persists locally in 'Barton Shop' and 'Barton Road'.

LOCATION

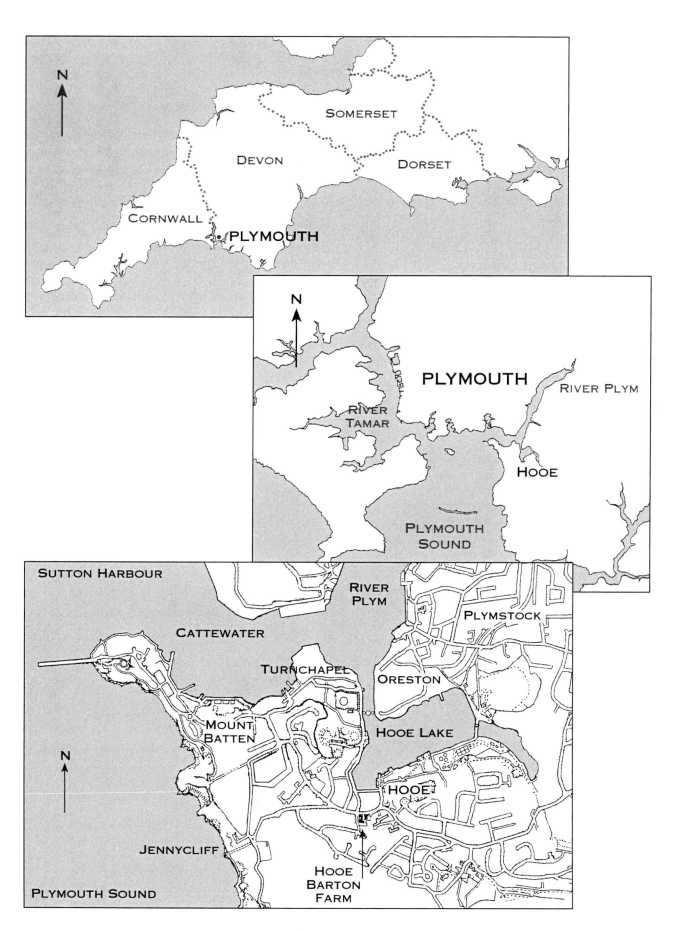

A Brief History

It is the 13th March 1967. Edna Sherrell is selling Hooe Barton Farm and most of the surrounding fields to G. Wimpey and Sons, builders. She owns the farm, which she lets out, and is retiring from her career as a florist in Plymouth to live in Tenby, Wales. So will end a continuous history of over 800 years during which the Farm was the central player in the life and development of Hooe.

Hooe Lake is a sheltered inlet just off the Cattewater and nearly opposite the original port of Plymouth. The Cattewater, which is the estuary of the Plym, is a natural harbour sheltered from the South West gales by the peninsular of Mount Batten. So Hooe Lake is a most convenient, sheltered watering, victualling and trading place. It has a constant fresh water supply at the southern end and a manor that could supply milk, fruit and vegetables. Being tidal it is also a good place to beach a vessel for routine maintenance and the nearby village of Turnchapel provided boat building and repair services aplenty.

Geologically the lake is a fault in a band of Devonian limestone that curves from Mount Edgecombe through Plymouth (forming the Hoe) to Yealmpton and is thought to be the remains of a huge prehistoric atoll. Before quarrying carved much of the surrounding shoreline Hooe would have been of much different appearance, see cover. The hills would have run to tree covered bluffs on the shores of the lake. The narrow entrance from the Cattewater would have been more dramatic than at present with cliffs or steep hills rising rapidly to 200ft on the western side from the narrow cleft of water. The shoreline is likely to have been rough and steep at this point as the main access to Turnchapel went over the hill rather than the shorter route around the shore. Once through the entrance the lake would open up to a sheltered harbour surrounded by fields, pastures and tree lined hills. Though the lake was probably tidal it was much less silted up than at present and so deep water was available for longer periods.

Hooe Manor was situated on the southern shore of Hooe Lake and occupied the site of the original Saxon Manor House of Hooe, which is mentioned in Domesday. To be significant enough to be included it must have developed previously and there is archaeological evidence that there has been a settlement at Hooe since Neolithic times. It would be a most favourable location too with shelter from gales, a reliable water supply, arable land, ease of access to the sea and something of a sun trap. Initially land access would be difficult, the surrounding hills are steep and one would need to travel some way up the River Plym to cross at Marsh Mills before being able to reach points west, but in a maritime area transport is by boat and the land only figures for short journeys until road access, bridge or ferry provision improves.

Over the years settlement and trade increased and Hooe Manor also grew in size, its lands extending around and over the surrounding hills. Initially owned by the Priors of Plympton and let to a range of tenants it became an important trading and victualling place.

It was important enough to be granted a licence to build a small chapel within the manor complex (variously called St. Laurence's chapel or St. Anne's Chapel) and later to hold services there.

Being isolated it was quite heavily protected and the earliest known picture of the Manor in 1694 (below) shows a substantially fortified building.

Hooe Manor by J. Spoure 1694. If the date is accurate then it shows Hooe Barton Farm after it has been restored following the Civil War. What appears to be a chapel is situated within the central dividing wall, though it may be of some other purpose. The Elizabethan Barn is clearly identifiable on the left as is Shute Quay (1) and Hooe village (2). The large sailing ship is more a product of decoration than accuracy. Reproduced by permission of the trustees.

During the Civil War it was one of the local centres of Royalist activity until the Roundheads sailed into Hooe Lake and opened fire on it, substantially modifying its structure and curtailing its Royalist functions.

After the war the manor was rebuilt but more as a farm than a fortified manor. Perhaps because of the wave of Puritanism that swept the country, or because the Roundheads had irreversibly modified it, the small chapel was demolished and the sole remaining arch was incorporated into the rebuilding to form a gateway between the outer and inner courtyards. The barn also survived. Despite all this Hooe Barton Farm retained its importance as a victualling and trading place; it would have been the main employer in the area and the centre of this community.

The farm grows in size and importance until the mid 1800's when it occupies 242 acres. The decline sets in just after the turn of the 19th century. The farm fields are hilly and unsuitable for mechanisation, labour is getting more expensive and it is difficult to compete with farms that *have* mechanised. Transport is becoming more efficient. Refrigeration is improving, owners are getting older and wanting to realise their assets. Perhaps the Bayly's saw the writing on the wall when they sold to Ernest and George Sherrell. The first few years of their ownership are successful and they work the farm themselves. Then they retire and let it to Winnie and Jack Ford.

One might say that the Sherrell brothers are either the major architects of the decline or the victims of circumstances. During their tenure foot and mouth and the war occur, new milk (TT) regulations are introduced and competition becomes more intense. To help out financially parts of the farm land are sold off piecemeal. Some land for the shop, the garage, the MoD pumping station, Westway for housing, Homer Hamacre for housing and finally Edna Sherrell, the last surviving child, sells the remaining property.

Efforts to save from demolition the oldest portion of the farm buildings, the Elizabethan barn, are successful. Although far less successful are the subsequent attempts to utilise it or even undertake basic maintenance. It remains today, surrounded on two sides by an undistinguished shopping precinct, the victim of neglect by its owners Plymouth City Council, unless...

FARM BUILDINGS AND USE

In 1995 Richard Tidmarsh, Senior Economic Planning Officer for Plymouth City Council, undertook an evaluation of Hooe Barton Farm and the Barn in particular.

His plan below is based on the 1866 OS Map (page 14) supplemented by recollections from those who lived and worked in the area.

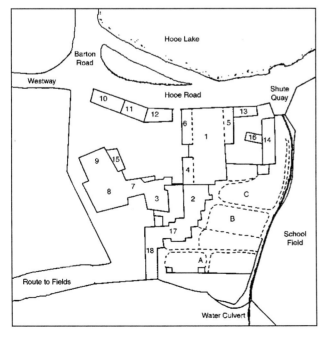

KEY   Items in bold type survive today

1   **Hooe Barn**
2   *Farmhouse*
3   *Dairy*
4   **West Shippon** *(for milking)*
5   **East Shippon** *(Palace Court)*
6. *Original use not known (probably shippon but by the beginning of 20th Century vehicle garage, monumental mason and store)*
7. *Shippon (4 cattle)*
8. *Shippon (7 cattle)*
9. *Stables*
10, 11, 12.   *These were used for storage and appear to have been shippons previously, because of their location there may have been an earlier connection with the production of cider. Demolished C1890.*
13, 14. *Cow houses*
15, 16. *Dung pits*
17. *Bank Barn (original barn). Ruins by the end of the 19th century.*
18. *Not known (possibly second barn for alternative crop)*

AREAS
A) *Pigs, Poultry, Fruit trees etc.*
B) *Farmhouse garden*
C) *Farmhouse garden*

CHRONOLOGY

1086

Hooe is mentioned in the Domesday Book identifying it as 'Juhel has a Manor called Ho, which Alebrix held on the day King Edward was alive and rendered it geld for one virgate to Stephen. There is land sufficient for two ploughs, five acres of pasture and it is worth 20 shillings a year.'

In addition to the Manor, Stephen has land of his own: 'half a virgate and one plough'. A virgate was a quarter of a Hide. A Hide could be anything between 120 and 240 acres, it is not a measured area but a conjectural area used for Domesday tax purposes. The physical size is variable and depends upon the nature and quality of the land. It is related to a 'plough' which is the amount of land one plough drawn by a team of eight oxen could work in one day. Half a virgate was between 15 and 30 acres or 6 to 12 Hectares. The Manor lands were extensive and also included one saltwork, one fishery and woodland.

1166

Wido de Bocland, who has inherited Hooe Manor, makes it over to the Prior of Plympton. Wido now receives it back as a perpetual tenant at a rent of about 3 shillings a year.

1201

Alan de Bocland succeeds Wido, formally acknowledges the ownership of the Manor to be that of the Priors and the tenancy is transferred to him in on the same terms.

1238

Alan's daughter, Isabella, complains to the court in Exeter that Prior Robert, who is new to his post, is not honouring the agreement made between her father and the previous Prior. She wins her case and Prior Robert agrees that Isabella and her heirs should hold the manor forever.

Isabella marries Osbert Giffard and the tenancy continues in the Giffard family until...

1306

There is a quarrel between the brothers Ralph and Osbert Giffard, both of whom claim Hooe Manor. The case is taken to court at Westminster where Osbert acknowledges Ralph's right to the Manor and Ralph agrees to Osbert's possession until Osbert dies, when the ownership will revert to Ralph and not pass to the descendants of Osbert.

1346

Ralph Giffard sublets the Manor to John Bernard. From this time onwards the tenancy changes many times as various sublettings are undertaken.

1350 (CIRCA)

A small private Chapel is built at the Manor and probably called St. Laurence's Chapel (see page 31).

1387

The Plympton Priory is granted the right to hold religious services in St. Laurence's chapel.

1403

John Brackler, the current tenant, is granted his own license to have religious services performed in his 'mansions at Plympton and Westhoobray.'

1480 (CIRCA)

The manor is leased by Sir William Paulet for 6 shillings and 8 pence per year (33 new pence).

1488

Sir William Paulet gives the Manor to his nephew Amyas Paulet.

1500

Sir William Paulet dies.

Around this time important trading centres around Plymouth become known as 'Palaces'. Plymouth merchants of the time commonly use the term Palace to describe their living and trading centres. The name is believed to be derived from the Italian 'Palazzo'. Their construction is typically that of storage and trading facilities near to road or water transport. The first edition Ordnance Survey map (1855), shows the area immediately to the south of Hooe Village (now occupied by The Royal Oak) as a 'Palace' and the site between Hooe Barton Farm and Shute Quay as 'Palace Court'. These Palaces are particularly unusual as they are so far outside the town of Plymouth. The area on the east side of the barn including the east shippon itself is still known as Palace Court.

1539

Plympton Priory was dissolved and the Manor became the property of the Crown who let it for 8 shillings a year.

1558-1600

Elizabethan period. It is thought that the barn is built during this time to replace an older Bank Barn

Continued on page 11

A LOCAL TRADING DIFFICULTY

Evidence from Serjeant Hele's Precedent Book. 1593 - 1601 (in Plymouth Municipal Records by R.N.Worth Esq., Plymouth 1893), that Hooe Palace Merchants were trading in pilchards, though in this case not without argument.

Complaint of Thomas Ford, of Howe, Plymstock, Merchant. Touching his sale of pilchards to Symon Lucas, a merchant stranger of Nants in Little Britton. Sold four score and ten barrels for fourscore and 1 pounds delivered at Howe. Anthony Goddard of Plymouth has goods and money of Lucas and has been told to pay but refuses.
Goddard, or Guttard, denies this and does not see "why he should pay money when he oweth none."

Pilchards were laid into the barrels in circular layers and packed around with salt. There was a brisk pilchard trade with France, particularly to Brittany and Nantes has long been a fishing centre and importer of fish.

Much of the local catches were packed in pilchard cellars across the Sound at Cawsand and Kingsand.

A score is 20 so 'four score and ten' is 90 and 'four score and one' is 81. He sold 90 barrels for £81.

A barrel contained just over 31 gallons (119 litres). This size was typical of those used for pilchard packing at the time although occasionally a hogshead barrel of 63 gallons (238.5 litres) was used.

A TRUE MAPP AND DESCRIPTION OF THE TOWNE. 1643

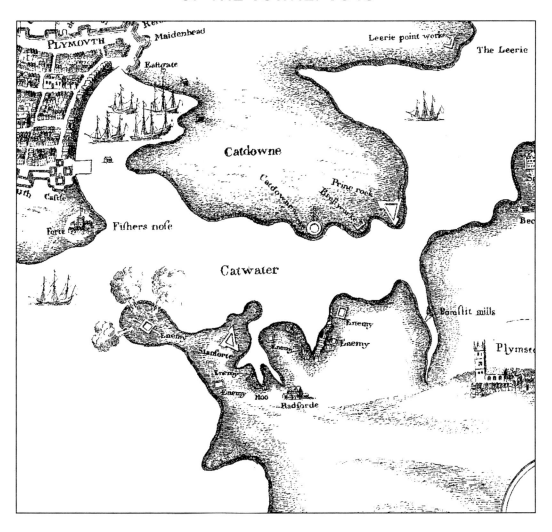

This is a detail of a well known Parliamentarian map, reprints and versions of which are available from map dealers and antique shops. It was drawn to show 'the fortifications thereof, with the workes and approaches of the Enemy at the last seige' during the Civil War. The 'enemy' are the Royalists. Hooe Lake seems to have had another branch off it to the west but judging by the general lack of accuracy it is probably a mistake. At that point there was a solid limestone hill about 31 metres high that would later be quarried away. Hooe itself is given some attention graphically.

TITHE MAP 1840/42

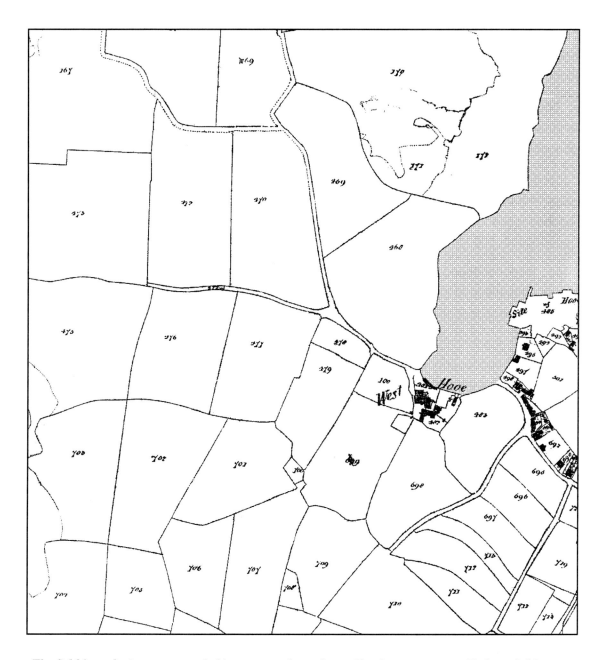

The field boundaries stay remarkably constant throughout all subsequent maps. Notice a field access road or track running in from Hooe Road. The upper entrance to Hooe Primary School now follows this in part and it is interesting to follow the fate of this road over the following maps.

This copy has been cleaned up to remove creases, microfilm scratches and photocopier noise so it should not be assumed to be totally accurate. Reproduction with permission from Plymouth and West Devon Record Office.

in the hillside behind the manor, possibly by Thomas Forde the current tenant. The barn is used initially as a threshing barn and it is this which makes it especially rare. There are thought to be only three others in the country. Built to take advantage of the natural draft from the prevailing westerly winds corn or barley would be deposited in the centre of the barn and the draft across the threshing floor would help remove the chaff. In later years a threshing machine was installed in the north end.

1585

Thomas Forde is Mayor of Plymouth for one year. To celebrate his mayordom he has one of the courtyards paved with pebbles in which are heraldic patterns including the Plymouth coat of arms.

1631

The Court of Augmentations, who were established to dispose of former monastic lands, sell the manor to Richard Forde.

1642

The Civil War begins (1642-1646). The Plymouth area is strongly Royalist and the manor at the head of the lake is a Royalist stronghold.

1643

Richard Forde dies.
October 8th. Commanded by Colonels Wardlaw and Gould a Parliamentarian force sail up Hooe Lake and attack the manor, which is severely damaged in the process. They capture 50 men and a quantity of ammunition. It is likely that the chapel is either destroyed then or in the wave of Puritanism that rolls through the Civil War and the period immediately afterwards. The barn survives and the site is rebuilt more as a farm than a manor. All that remains of the old chapel, a granite arched doorway, is incorporated into the new buildings to form a gateway between the inner and outer courtyards.

1691

Judith Forde marries Captain Ralph Burrow.

1700 (CIRCA)

The Manor passes into the hands of the Rogers family who are distinguished and powerful local merchants. It does not seem that they live there but are letting it out to tenant farmers.

The farm prospers and grows. The fields are hilly and steep but plentiful labour at reasonable cost means that they are economic to work. Transport is mainly by water, Hooe Lake still comes nearly to the wall of the barn and Shute Quay juts out into the lake.

1736

Lady Rogers builds cottages in Yonder Street, Hooe village.

Detail of print by S. Prout, 1810, (See inside back cover) showing the farm and gable end of the Barn at the southern end of Hooe Lake. Shute Quay is evident and there appears to be a structure over where the water flows out from the Brakes.

1842

The tithe map of 1840/42 (Page 10) shows Barton Farm with 242 acres (98hectares) and let to John Hart. It is an exceptionally large farm for its day.

11

1843

The parish map of the Hooe area is produced which includes field names. (See page 13).

1861

Building commences on Staddon and Stamford Forts. A main water supply pipe is laid between the two forts crossing the farm land. Building is completed in 1870.

1871

The census shows Philip and Mary Ann Hine at Hooe Barton Farm. It is probable that they were tenant farmers.

1872

The farm is now in the posession of John Bayly and family who are important and wealthy Plymouth timber merchants supplying timber for boat building and railway sleepers.

1881

Philip and Mary Ann Hine's son, Philip Bluett Hine, marries Mary Susan Reid. The parents, Philip and Mary, move to Courtgates Farm at Staddiscombe. Philip Bluett and Mary Susan Hine run Hooe Barton Farm as tenant farmers.

1893.

John Bayly dies and the farm passes to his heirs to be operated as a trust.

Philip Bluett and Mary Susan Hine. Photograph collection of Mary Outhwaite, whose grandparents they are.

Hooe Lake and Village circa 1900.
The line of trees in the foreground is the edge of what will be Amacre Drive.

PARISH MAP 1843

This fascinating map shows all the field names, many of which have roots far in the past and are the source of present day names. Starting at Hooe Barton Farm, labelled 'Hooe', to the west is West, from which we get 'Westway' (not spelled with an 's' on the end, the current road sign is inaccurate).

To the north east is Homer Hamacre, derived from The Home Acre, the acre field closest to the farm at time of naming. This survives in Amacre Drive.

To the east of the farm 'Penny Park', now occupied by Hooe School, is derived from the Celtic 'Pen y cwm cuig' Translated as 'where the creek meets the end of a valley' (Barber 1999).

Four fields due south from Penny Park is Higher Hingstone. Ivy Langdon states that in 1967 two large stones, about five feet high by two (1.5 x 0.61 metres) were discovered in the farmyard and thought to be standing stones that had been removed from their original site. As one of the nearby fields was called Higher Hingstone, a name with Neolithic roots, this gave weight to the standing stone theory. Unfortunately they disappeared during the building work that was just starting.

ORDNANCE SURVEY
1ST EDITION. 1866

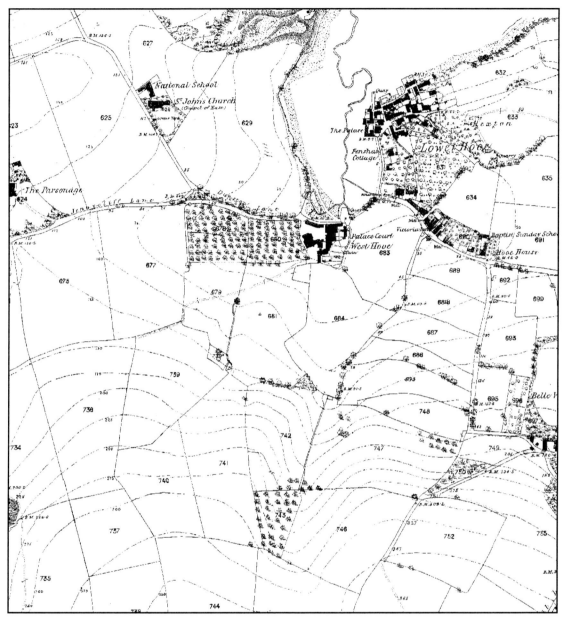

This detail shows some interesting features. The farm is drawn with what appears to be a line of buildings bordering the road in front of the main farmyard. There is an irregular structure by the rear garden running due south from the Farm House. Richard Tidmarsh is of the opinion that it is, in part, the remains of the old Bank Barn that was replaced by present Elizabethan Barn.

A sluice is shown in the farm garden where water that flowed from the reservoirs higher up the Brakes and came out at Shute Quay could be diverted for irrigating the garden.

On the west side, occupying the fields 'West', 'Higher Orchard' and part of 'Higher Meadow' (plots 678 and 680) the map shows as being set to trees, probably an orchard if the field name is a true description and may be connected with the production of cider.

The area on the east side of the farm is marked 'Palace Court' and there is another Palace in Hooe Village on the site of what is now the beer garden of the Royal Oak public house.

Immediately in front of the farm Hooe Lake comes close to the farm wall, about a single track road's width. The area which is now a small green with telephone boxes was tidal. Barton Road tracked through this to reach slightly higher ground. Amacre Drive will closely follow the 25 foot contour line.

ORDNANCE SURVEY
2ND EDITION
1894

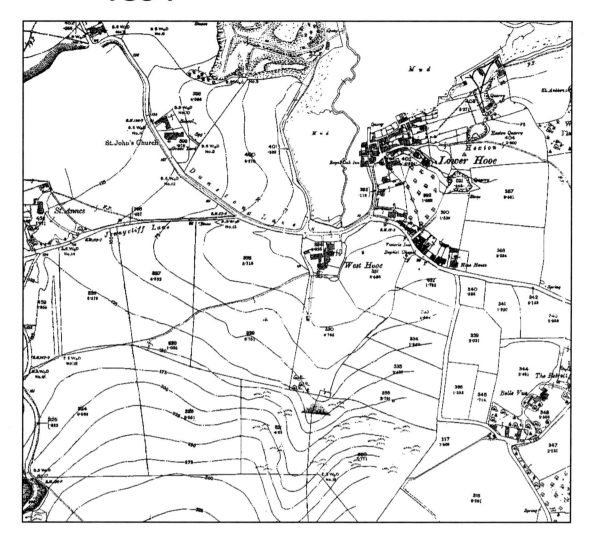

The small south west corner of the lake has been filled in recently according to this detail and the farm reservoir is now marked together with the culvert that supplied the dairy. The photograph on the back cover shows the farm at this time.

Fort Stamford is not shown because it is a defence structure and to show it might give information to an enemy.

OVERLEAF: In the intervening 40 years or so since the 1894 OS Map there has been more building. Homer Hamacre shows Amacre Drive and part of St John's Drive. Buildings marked black exist at the time, those in outline are in the process of being built or permission has been given to build. Lake Stores is now shown just to the east of the farm.

Dunstone Lane has been renamed Church Hill Road. The reason for the renaming has yet to be discovered.

The school has appeared and the farm reservoir is marked by the 50ft contour behind the farm.

*The Barton Road entrance has been tidied up. This the Hooe that **Claude Dampier** would have seen.*

ORDNANCE SURVEY
1933 REVISED 1938

BELOW:
Edna Sherrell's wedding to her first husband, Arthur Jarrold, on the 1st June 1936 at Hooe Church.

1. Edna Sherrell
2. Arthur Jarrold
3. Elva Peard, Edna's cousin
4. Edith Sherrell, Edna's mother
5. Mrs Peard, Elva's mother
6. Elva Peard's brother
7. Ivy Tucker. Later married Alfie Williams
8. Henry Jarrold, Arthur's father
9. Agnes Jarrold, Arthur's mother
10. Jack Jarrold, Arthur's brother
11. Grace Jarrold, Arthur's sister
12. Hilda Olver, Arthur's sister
13. Ernest Sherrell, Edna's father
14. George Sherrell, Edna's uncle
15. John Olver, age five
16. George Jarrold, Arthur's brother

Edna's sister, Dorothy, may have been too ill to attend. She had TB and died five months later. Arthur contracted TB and died two years later on the 26th December 1938.

Photograph courtesy of John Symons

1918

By the end of the first World War the farm had shrunk to 70 acres. Mechanisation, which improved farm productivity, was not suitable for the hilly fields. The cost of labour and land increased.

1920

23rd November. Ernest (Ernie) Sherrell buys Hooe Farm from Karl Daman of Wallingford, Berks and Alfred John Meybohm Venning of Plymouth (both of whom are husbands of Bayly daughters and trustees of the estate) for £3,550. Ernest is 42 at the time, his wife Edith is 37. They have two daughters: Dorothy, the eldest, then 15 and Edna, who later opens florist shops in Plymouth. See **Bayly to Sherrell** for more detail.

1926

November. The mortgage was discharged, probably helped by selling Homer Hamacre field to Clare Elford and Plot No.326 (currently the football field at Jennycliff) to Mrs. E A Coates, the wife of Colonel Coates who lived in Hooe Manor (Belle Vue). The name Homer Hamacre survives through Amacre Drive.

1930

27th January. Airship R100 flies over Hooe on a trial trip.

1931 (Circa)

Mrs. Winifred Tapper leases a piece of the Farmyard next to Shute Quay from Ernest Sherrell. She employs Crockers, builders at Goosewell, to build a small shop and living accommodation called 'Harwin', a name derived from the first names of Harry and Winifred Tapper. See **The Lake Stores.**

1932 (Circa)

All the cows on the Farm are diagnosed as having Foot and Mouth. The entire herd of twenty South Devons are shot in the Barn, their carcasses dragged up to a large pit, burned and buried in quicklime, (now somewhere under Pollard Close). There would have been compensation for the price of each cow but for no other associated costs. Given that this was a dairy herd the financial effect would have been instantaneous and severe.

1933

13th February. Mrs Tapper opens her shop, known locally as 'Tappers'.
7th March. Winifred Tapper buys the freehold of the land for £60.

Hooe Post Office and a neighbouring shop, a butchers, are built in Lake Road. Mrs Perry opens the Post Office, Mr Stevens opens the butchers.

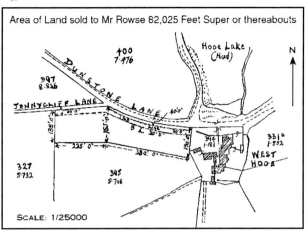

Map from conveyance document, Sherrell to Rowse

1935.

Mr C. W. Rowse purchases a plot of land running up the south side of Church Hill, called Westway (after the original field) for £900. The large elms that line the south side of the road are cut down. Nos 3 & 4 Westway are the first houses to be built. He occupies No. 4 and his sister No. 3. Gradually other houses are completed up the hill, ending with Nos 1 and 2 at the bottom. The reason for the odd building sequence might be because Rowse knew that building was due to commence on the pumping station and so he delays until it is completed.

A strip of land around the north and east walls of the Barn is sold to Mr. Hercules Doddridge who intends building a garage and filling station for his son Hedley to run.
See **Hooe Barton Garage & Shop** on page 50.

1936

24th November. Dorothy Sherrell dies aged 31.

1938

20th August. Film and radio comedians Claude Dampier and Billie Carlyle park their white, custom made, Fairway caravan in the orchard at the rear of the farm while appearing at the Palace Theatre in Plymouth. Not only are they great celebrities but they have an unique caravan.
See **Claude Dampier** on page 61.

1939

23rd February. Wimpey start excavations next to Hooe Barton Farm for an MoD aviation fuel pumping station and holding tank. It is likely that this was compulsorily purchased under war emergency regulations. The pipeline runs from Turnchapel Wharves, along Barton Road to the farm and up over Hooe Hill to the fuel depot in Radford Woods. Tankers moored at Turnchapel wharves pump the fuel to this station from where it is pumped onwards to Radford Oil Fuel Depot. From here it is taken by

Continued on page 20

17

Hooe Lake 1930 taken from a position close to where the 1813 P.H. Rogers painting was made. (See inside cover). Photograph collection of Mary Skilton.

Hooe 1933 photographed from the Brakes immediately behind Hooe Barton Farm. Photograph collection of Joan Phillips.

Hooe Village circa 1948. Photograph collection of June Whyte.

Hooe Lake circa 1950.

RAF Area Map. 1940

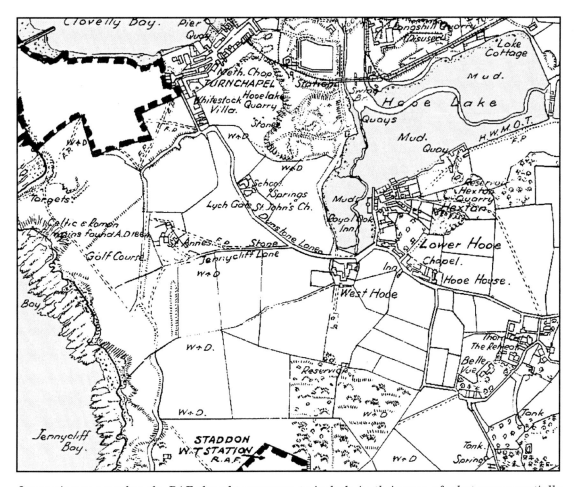

Interesting to see what the RAF thought necessary to include in their map of what was essentially Mount Batten (not shown on this detail). They have marked the Celtic and Roman finds site at Dunstone Point. The newly named Church Hill Road is referred to by its original name. Bayly's reservoir is marked, tucked up in the corner of the large field behind the farm, as is the farm's reservoir complete with culvert to the dairy. The small plot of land to the west of the Farm is the MoD pumping station, which is in the process of being built.

road to the Royal Naval Air Bases at Yeovilton and Culdrose after cleaning and blending. (Parts of the pipeline exist at time of writing.)

March (circa). Henry and Winifred Tapper move to Oreston and the village shop is leased by Josephine and Stephen Mahon who name it **The Lake Stores.**

1940

January 12th onwards. The pipeline from Turnchapel Wharf to Radford is completed and tested.

24th August. The newly completed and tested pipeline leaks petrol into Hooe Lake. Some catches fire and is put out. All cars and pedestrians are stopped to warn against smoking until repairs are completed.

28th November. Eleven high explosive and seven incendiary bombs fall in the field adjoining Westway. Houses are damaged and a garage is demolished.

Sometime this year Ernie Sherrell lets the Farm to Jack and Wynnie Ford.

Railings are fitted around the southern end of Hooe Lake from Barton Road junction to the Post Office. Welsh Fusiliers and 5th Devon troops are stationed in tents and temporary buildings behind the farm to guard the oil tanks at Turnchapel and Radford.

1941

21st March. 1 HE bomb falls in the field near Hooe School and 1 HE bomb in West Hooe Farm with damage to farm, barn and nearby houses. Rastus the billy goat dies from fright. Damage to troop's accommodation.

1943

20th October. The barrage balloon, which has been tethered in the field behind the school, gets out of control, comes down by the farmhouse, explodes and catches part of the house on fire.

1947

Nos 1 & 2 Westway sold for £3,600 to Mr M.R. Morrow.

1948

6th February. Ernest Sherrell dies, aged 70.

1950

The west shippon, which was used as a milking parlour for three cows, is cement rendered to comply with TT regulations. The work carried out by Mr. Stevens who worked for H. Hockin, plumbers and builders.

1951

Mrs Tapper leases Lake Stores to Doreen Glinn. The Mahons leave to live and work in Plymouth. See **The Lake Stores** page 44.

1956

September/October. Mobilisation for suez war. Desert camouflaged tanks are parked along Barton Road prior to embarkation at Sycamore Beach, Turnchapel. Troops asking for teas from Lake Stores.

1964

February. Work started on infilling the southern end of Hooe Lake. A wall of caged stone is built straight across from the Royal Oak to the opposite bank. Infill comes from Hay Quarry, Stag Lodge and debris from houses demolished in Hooe Village, under the slum clearance scheme and also from Plymouth Harvest Home and Breakwater Quarry, Oreston. The latter gives space for the new gas works. Pipes are laid to culvert water from Shute Quay and the south west corner of the lake by Westway into Hooe Lake.

1965

24th February. Edith Sherrell dies aged 82. The farm passes to Edna Sherrell, her daughter.
1st September. Doreen Glinn buys the freehold of The Lake Stores from Winifred Tapper for £3,500.

1966

It becomes known that the farm is for sale and that George Wimpey are interested in purchasing it and surrounding fields, which have outline planning permission for development as housing, with shop development in the farm. The Civic Society and the Old Plymouth Society voice their concerns over the future of the barn and arch.

1967

27th February. Railings alongside fields in Jennycliff Road are removed and house building on the fields commences.

Hooe Barton Farm in 1968.
Photo: Stanley Goodman, collection of Sheila Coleman.

13th March. John Daman, Alfred Venning and Edna Sherrell complete the sale of the Farm and surrounding fields for £38,025 to George Wimpey, builders. A rectangle of land that includes the farm reservoir is not included in the sale.
24th August. First of Wimpey's houses occupied. (Pollard Close)
25th October. It is reported that two standing stones, first seen by Mr Eric Lord with Mr Turpin from the planning authority, had been removed from the farm.

1968

Spirited local concern, with the support of the Old Plymouth Society, results in an application for the barn to be protected as a listed building. Wimpey put a new roof on the barn. Good slates but inferior nails.

1969

15th September. Farmhouse and outbuildings demolished. The wooden door to the arch disappears as does the circular stone apple crusher by the main gate.

28th October. The Barn is listed as Grade 2.

1970

The land occupied by the farmhouse and outbuildings is sold to Keedollan Properties.

25th March. The Hooe and Turnchapel Community Association lease the barn from Wimpey for a peppercorn rent of £5pa. The Association hope they can raise the money necessary to renovate it and put it to community use as it is apparent that Wimpey are doing little with it.

The Association trustees approach Miller Williams, architects, to draw up plans for converting the barn into a community centre. Plans and a schedule are drawn up to enable developers to tender for the conversion but nothing comes of it.

1971

Keedollan properties build the present shop units with flats over. The original plan was for the whole of the ground floor of the building across the South side to be a Co-op Supermarket with storage upstairs served by a goods lift at the eastern end. Halfway through construction the Co-op pull out saying that their plans are now for bigger units. For some time no-one would take the space; it remained boarded up and a target for vandalism. Later it was divided into five individual shop units of which two are currently let.

1979

A notice under the Public Health Act is served on Wimpey by PCC regarding the state of the Barn and requiring them to replace slates, rooflights, guttering, repair the crack in south wall corner and remove plants growing from walls. This was not done. Technically this notice may still remain in force.

11th October. Letter to Wimpey from Stanley Goodman noting that a Cider Mill-House, with cider press, adjacent to the Barn had disappeared.

1980

27th November. From City Council Minutes: 'The Hooe Barton and District Air Weapons Club wish to use the Barn as their club premises. The Planning Committee has made a grant of £4,286 towards the cost of conversion subject to the repairs being satisfactorily carried out.'
No repairs or alterations are done and the Weapons Club do not use the premises. See **Newspaper Reports** page 67.

1982

One of the shop units is rented by Mr and Mrs Wheeler and run as a fruit/vegetable and health food shop, called Strawberry Fayre, until 1989 when they retire. Several other tenants follow continuing the fruit and vegetable business.

20th October. The Hooe and Turnchapel Community Association can no longer support the running repairs and insurance premiums. They assign the lease to Plymouth City Council for £1. PCC then purchase the Barn from Wimpey for £150.

1983

9th September. Mr Beddows of 21 Fisher Road, Milehouse, Plymouth expresses an interest in purchasing the Barn. PCC offer it to him for £3,500 but the sale does not proceed.

1988

Doreen Glinn retires. The Lake Stores is bought by Plymouth City Council and leased to William McMonagle. Later this will be occupied by a second-hand car business and Tony Kelway (Hooe Pasties).

1995/96

The conservation group 'Radford and Hooe Lake Preservation Association' make a serious attempt to lease the barn from Plymouth City Council in order to repair and restore it and bring it into use. PCC proposed a 6 yr lease at a peppercorn rent, the Association to be responsible for repairs and insurance with no sub-letting. The Association hope to make application for National Lottery funding but discover that at least a 25 yr lease is required before funding can be considered.

However, they obtain two grants from Plymouth Development Corporation Community Chest small grants fund, a total of £1,500.
This money is used to clear the interior of the barn, removing a mobile classroom that PCC had stored there for years and to clear the area at the rear of the barn. This was done in order that an initial survey could be carried out by two professional surveyors (retired), work done without charge.

Internal work involved two men and a lorry, eight days work, seven hours per day with eighteen lorryloads to the tip.
External work involved two men and a lorry, six days work at seven hours per day and fifteen lorryloads to the tip.
Total cost £1,568.

Regrettably after all their work the Association decided that without Lottery funding they could not take the lease.

1999

The situation of neglect and disinterest over the Barn concerns the local community and following a public meeting on 13th May the 'Friends of Hooe Barn' was formed to act as a pressure group and agent of change.

A website is created. Several meetings are held with Planning and Surveyors dept. of PCC, local councillors, Gary Streeter MP and Groundwork Trust to discuss the immediate repairs needed and future

Friends of Hooe Barn meeting with PCC outside Hooe Barn. L to R: John Emery, Mary Outhwaite, Geoff O'Neill (PCC), Sheila Coleman, John Vare (PCC Lottery), Kay Marks, Tudor Evans (Leader PCC), Cllr. Ruth Earl, Mary Skilton.

development. A questionnaire is put in the local shop to gain public views on possible use and funding sources are investigated.

3rd December. Following a site visit from PCC Surveyors the rear chimney is said to be dangerous and needs shortening and capping 'as a matter of great urgency'.

Students surveying inside the Barn

2000

17th February. Second year students from the School of Civil and Structural Engineering, Plymouth University, undertake a brief to devise innovative and creative solutions for converting the barn to use or uses suggested by the community.

They present their designs on Wednesday 17th May 2000 at the Friends of Hooe Barn. AGM.

Following this the designs are put on public display and members of the public are invited to vote on their preferences. The result is that a conversion to an Art/Craft & Interpretation Centre is the most popular choice.
The Friends of Hooe Barn contact the Pro Help Group (a group of local architects and surveyors who advise on community projects) and they agree to look at the feasibility of the proposal.

Roof slates are still needing replacement.

2001

January. A few slates are replaced in the easier to reach lower areas of the roof.

February. Some of the recently replaced slates fall off together with more from other areas.

April. Further slate slips. The dangerous chimney, noted by PCC in December 1999 'as a matter of great urgency', remains untouched.

The Pro Help Group report back to the Friends of Hooe Barn. The proposal is viable, the barn can be sympathetically converted for this use.

11th May. Alderman Tom Savery unveils the Hooe Barn Plaque which commemorates the barn and Archway.

The plaque inscription reads:

HOOE BARN and ARCHWAY
The only surviving remains of West Hooe Farm,
centre of the ancient Manor of Hooe,
first recorded in the Domesday book of 1086,
and of the chapel of St. Laurence
founded within the 14th Century Manor.
The Archway could have formed part of either
the Manor House or Chapel.

The Threshing Barn is Elizabethan.

The Farmhouse, parts of which were 16th Century
and built on the site of the Manor House,
adjoined the Barn on the southern side,
was demolished in 1969.

The Barn was saved by the Old Plymouth Society.

BAYLY TO SHERRELL. THE DETAILS...

FARM PLAN 1920

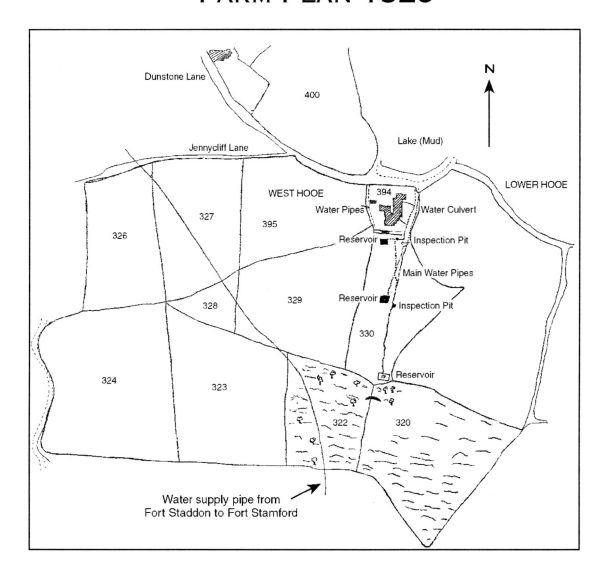

Hooe Barton Farm as bought by Ernest Sherrell from the Baylys in November 1920. The reservoir marked closest to the farm might be inacurrate as it cannot be remembered by those who worked at the farm in its later years. The centre reservoir fed the Farm Dairy milk cooler and the top reservoir fed Shute Quay and some was used for farm garden irrigation.

None of the reservoirs were sold to Ernest Sherrel. The Baylys kept ownership as they needed a fresh water supply for their timber yard at the entrance to Hooe Lake.

When Edna Sherrell sold the farm to Wimpey she could not sell the reservoirs because they were not hers to sell.

1872

11th December. John Bayly, owner of the farm, makes his will. On his death the farm is to be run as a trust by and for the benefit of his surviving children, his brothers and sisters-in-law and their children. Their coming of age (25 years), or upon marriage, entitles them to become a trustee and administer the farm.

1876

20th February. John Bayly makes an indenture with Rt. Hon. Frederick Baron Blatchford, Secretary of State for War that concerns various restrictions of use in favour of the War Office. These particularly refer to the War Office having certain rights of access over Jennycliff Lane and requiring restrictions on certain types of buildings and livestock in neighbouring fields. These are connected with the access, maintenance and firing lines of Staddiscombe and Stamford Forts as well as the water main that runs between them. *(About two thirds of Plymouth was affected by these at the time because of the Palmerston Forts. All have now been rescinded).*

1893

22nd July. John Bayly dies having had six children:
Robert Bayly the elder
Richard Bayly the elder (who died in 1875)
Agnes Bayly
Anna Bayly
Marianne Daman
Elizabeth Venning

16th November. The will is proved and following a civil court case (Bayly v Bayly 1894 B 4342) in 1895 the farm passes to the trustees who now consisted of
Robert Bayly the elder
Agnes Bayly
Anna Bayly
Elizabeth Venning
Marianne Daman

1901

18th July. Robert Bayly the elder dies. He has eight children, all of whom attain 25 yrs of age.
Agnes Emma Bayly
Edith Anna Bayly
Elizabeth Mary Bayly
Emily Bayly
John Bayly the younger
Katherine Margaret Bayly
Richard Bayly the younger
Robert Bayly the younger

1903

2nd March. A deed poll in which the five female children: Agnes Emma Bayly, Edith Anna Bayly, Elizabeth Mary Bayly, Emily Bayly, and Katherine Margaret Bayly waive their right of approval over the acts of the trustees.
30th October. Elizabeth Venning dies without children.
The trustees now comprise of
Agnes Bayly
Anna Bayly
Marianne Daman

1912

2nd March. Richard Bayly the younger dies.
20th March. The Trustees meet to make replacements for the deceased members. It is agreed the trustees should now comprise of:
Agnes Bayly
Anna Bayly
John Frederick Carl Daman (Marianne Daman's husband).
Robert Bayly the younger

1913

23rd June. Robert Bayly the younger dies.

1914

10th February. Trustees appoint John Bayly the younger and Alfred John Maybohm Venning to be trustees, the whole of which are now:
Agnes Bayly
Anna Bayly
John Frederick Carl Daman
John Bayly the younger
Alfred John Maybohm Venning

1915.

29th July. Agnes Bayly dies without having been married.

1917

12th February. Marianne Daman dies leaving six children all of whom are at least 25 years old and therefore eligible to approve actions of the Trustees.
John Frederick Carl Daman
Thomas Walter Alfred Daman
Harold Edgar Daman
Robert Ferdinand Daman
Karl Adolphus Daman
Elizabeth Marie Nolting (wife of Karl Heinrich Nolting).

1918

26th February. John Bayly the younger dies. The trustees now consist of:
Anna Bayly
John Frederick Carl Daman
Alfred John Maybohm Venning

1920

9th September. The trustees agree to sell the whole farm to Ernest Sherrell for £3,550.

However there was one continuing condition and a new, important exemption.

• The condition is the indenture with Rt. Hon. Frederick Baron Blatchford of 1876 that concerns various restrictions of land use in favour of the War Office, which is still in force.

• The exemption is the exclusion from the sale of the sites of two reservoirs and connecting pipes, with the right to take water from them and to enter upon the land to open, repair and maintain them retained by the Bayly's and their heirs. These reservoirs and pipes are in field 330.
The reservoirs collect ground water from the brakes and feed it down to Shute Quay via the farm garden and also to the water trough/milk cooler by the dairy. *(Until mains piped water arrived in Hooe the Shute Quay water supplied the village and had also been used for watering boats. However at least one supplied the Bayly's Timber Yard with water so they were properly concerned to retain control over the supply).*

Ernest Sherrell accepts these provisos and agrees not to interfere with the water supply nor to do anything to contaminate it. Furthermore he understands he would be compensated for any damage done by any maintenance and he will not be personally liable for any damages relating to the water supply either then, or after he had disposed of the property.

23rd November. In order to help pay for the farm Ernest Sherrell takes out a mortgage of £2,500 and pays the balance himself. The sale is completed.

At some time in this period Ernest Sherrell sells field 326 to Mrs E.A.Coates. It is now the football field at Jennycliff.

1926

4th October. The mortgage for £2,500 is discharged
5th October. Ernest Sherrell sells the Homer Hamacre field (No. 400) to William Henry Elford & Clarence Charles Elford for housing development.
6th October. Ernest Sherrell takes out a mortgage with Mrs M. A. Harvey for £500.
10th October. Ernest Sherrell purchases the Deed of Release from the conditions of the indenture with Rt. Hon. Frederick Baron Blatchford of 1876 relating to field 400.

1929

22nd June. The mortgage with Mrs Harvey for £500 is discharged.

6th July. Ernest Sherrell takes a mortgage with the Midland Bank for an unknown amount.

1935

27th September. Midland Bank mortgage is discharged.

1936

24th November. Dorothy Sherrell, eldest daughter, dies age 31.

28th September. Ernest Sherrell pays the War Department £400 for the Deed of Release from the conditions of the indenture with Rt. Hon. Frederick Baron Blatchford of 1876 relating to field 395. The purchaser is still liable to the War office for making good any damage he may do to that part of Jennycliff Lane that borders field 395 and contributing to its upkeep.

18th October. Ernest Sherrell sells part of Field 395 for housing development to Charles William Rowse, licensed victualler of The Victoria Inn, Hooe, for £900. Building commences on what is now known as Westway. (Note: The current road sign is spelled Westways. This is an error.)

1948

6th February. Ernest Sherrell dies age 70.

1965

24th November. Edith Sherrell dies age 82.

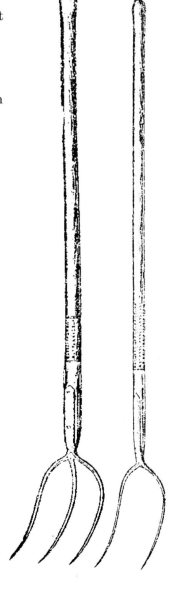

Estate Details 1813

In 1813 Hooe Barton Farm was put up for sale. The following is a description of the property for prospective purchasers. It is thought the Bayly family purchased it.

A Particular of the Manor Barton village of West Hooe within the Parish of Plymstock in the County of Devon.

The Barton consisting of an excellent Farm House Curtilages Barns Stables Linneys etc and 249 acres, 0 rods 24 poles be the same more or less of very good Orchard Meadow Pasture Village and Wood-

land with the privilege of Burning and Selling Lime but not Lime Stones now in the Occupation of Mr James Butland for the 14 years from Lady Day 1810 at the yearly rent of £395 0s .0p

The Tenant discharges all Outgoings except Landlords Property Tax and repairs everything except the Walls and other parts of the Dwelling House and the Walls Slate and Timber parts of the Roofs of the other Houses and Outhouses altogether not £10 a Year the same being all in good condition.

Liberty reserved to the Landlord to take any Grounds for the Purpose of building planting or otherwise using the same and of conducting any of the Streams of Water thereto and of destroying any of the present Buildings leaving sufficient or building others and of altering or making Roads making reasonable Satisfaction and other usual Reservations of Quarries etc.

	£	s	d
Net Rent of the Barton after deducting £10 for the above Repairs	385	0	0
Estimated worth more by great improvements at great Expense by parting several large Fields by Stone Walls and by extraordinary good Husbandry by the last Tenant at least	100	0	0
Estimated advantage by parting the Wellfield Part of the Barton into six Parts by Stone Walls to be let to Persons of Turnchapel about 17 acres from Christmas	49	10	0
Value of the soil of Coombe Wood and the Fir Plantation opposite	12	7	6
A large Dwelling House a little beyond Turnchapel in Possession of Sundry Tenants. It consists of 18 good Rooms with some Offices now let to a responsible Tenant for 3 years from Christmas 1812 clear of all Rates and Taxes at £60 allowing £5 per Annum for Repairs	55	0	0
Messrs John Rowse and Joseph Baker for a Lime Stone Quarry for 7 years from Lady Day 1808	12	12	0
The Same for a fresh Term of 7 years from Lady Day 1815 at the additional Rent of	11	8	0
Mr John Shepherd for another for the like former Time at	20	0	0
The Same for a fresh Term of 7 years from Lady Day 1815 at the additional Rent of	6	0	0
Mr William Pearse for another for the like former time at	21	0	0
The Same for a fresh Term of 7 years from Lady Day 1815 at the additional Rent of	6	0	0
Messrs Sparrow and Simons for another for the like former Time at	20	0	0
The same for a fresh Term of 7 years from Lady Day 1815 at the additional Rent of	6	0	0
Messrs Standon, Prinn and Wakeham for 3 ditto for 14 Years from Lady Day 1809 at	60	0	0
The same for a fresh Term of 7 Years at the additional Rent of	18	0	0
Mr James Butland another Quarry for 14 years from Lady Day 1813 at	20	0	0

As the Demand for Lime Stone is constantly increasing the Quarries become more and more valuable and the Lime Rock being of immense Extent and Quantity more Quarries may be let. The Tenants have built several Quays and are obliged to continue such Quays in Front of their Quarries and the space occasioned by working the Quarries being levelled with form an Extensive Area for building Houses, Warehouses etc. facing and communicating with the Quays with Gardens behind for which Liberty is reserved leaving sufficient Room for working the Quarries and carrying the Produce to the Quays — This has always been in the Contemplation of the Proprietor but the Quarries having been opened only a few Years sufficient Room is scarcely accomplished for this purpose.

Particulars of Hooe Village leased for 99 Years determinable on Lives

Names of Lessees	Names of Tenements	Names of Lives	Ages	Cond.ᵗ Rents	Quay Dues	Rents	Estimated neat yearly value
				s. d.	s. d.	s. d.	£. s. d.
Charles Fanshawe Esq.ʳ	Caenes 2 Tenements Gardens Orchards & Fields about 7 Acres let at £55 clear of every thing except Repairs of Walls and Roofs	Cha.ᵗ Fanshawe	71	none	none	none	60.0.0 65.0.0
William Hare Esq.ʳ	2 Fields about 3 Acres	Susanna Mills / Eliz.ᵗ Hare / Ann Buckel	54 / 54 / 41	5.0	1.6	63.0	15.0.0
Christian Bennett	Wetheridge's 2 Dwellings and Garden	Christ.ᵐ Bennett / Eliz.ᵗ Hendaw	62 / 27	3.6	1.6	2.6	7.0.0
Sarah Hawke	Hawkins's House and Garden	Sarah Hawke jun.ᵗ	35	6.0	1.6	2.0	8.0.0
The Same	Blake's House and Garden	Sarah Hawke jun.ᵗ	35				
John Hawke	3 Dwellings	Eliz.ᵗ Hawke / John Hawke	99 / 34	2.0	1.6	3.4	8.0.0
	Painters House & Garden	John Hawke	34	4.0	1.6	3.4	10.10.0
William Natt	Pines House & 2 Gardens	H. Wilkenson / Wm Natt / Sarah his wife	68 / 59 / 64	7.0	1.6	2.6	9.0.0
John Rouward late Jones widow / Matthew Horton	Burnard's two Dwellings & small Garden	John Rouward / his wife / R. Gribbel jun.ᵗ	32 / 27 / 15	3.4	1.6	3.4	8.8.0
	Warren's 2 Dwellings and Gardens	John Horton	47	6.0	1.6	3.4	5.0.0
Mary Curtis's Executors	Cornish's 2 Dwellings & Garden	Josias Curtis	37	8.0	1.6	3.4	8.8.0
Mess.ʳˢ King	Noxes the Public House	Elizab.ᵗ Tawke / John King / Richard King	46 / 26 / 22	4.0	1.6	5.0	20.0.0
Robert Coath	Clark's one good and a small House added and Garden	Robert Coath / R. P. Coath his son	52 / 31	8.0	1.6	3.4	15.0.0
John Taylor	Hingston's new House and Garden	Jn.º Taylor / Mary his wife / Jn.º their son	46 / 38 / 18	2.3			8.0.0
Samuel Way	Bowmans House and Garden	Sophia Colman / Susanna Way	26 / 28	2.0	1.6	2.0	5.10.0
Sam.ᵗ Way and John Trent late Martha Harry	Bryants (rebuilt) new two Houses	John Wyatt / Albert Trant	8 / 15	2.8	1.6	2.6	24.0.0
Robert Coath late J. Penrose	Part of Parnell House & Garden	Wm Coath / Tho.ˢ Coath / Kitty Coath	22 / 15 / 19	0.6	0.9	1.3	5.10.0
Charles Bennett	Other Part of Parnell 2 Houses and Quay opposite	Cha.ᵗ Bennett / Eliz.ᵗ his Wife / Ralph his son	55 / 57 / 22	0.6	0.9	1.3	20.0.0
Ann Elworthy	Welsh's 2 Houses 3 or 4 Dwellings & large Garden	Ann Elworthy / J. G. Cawley	69 / 43	3.0	1.6	1.8	9.7.0
The Same	Warren's House & Garden	Ann Elworthy	69	3.0	1.6	1.8	8.8.0
George Wyatt	Hart's Lower Tenement House Backlet and Quay	John Bawden	47	5.0	1.6	3.4	7.10.0
Samuel Warden	Cooly's House and large Garden	Sam.ᵗ Warden	53	3.6	1.6	3.4	17.0.0
Andrew Strathan	Sanders's House & Garden	Ruth Watson / Mary Hanson / Tobina Strathan	56 / 27 / 22	1.0	1.6	2.6	5.5.0
				40.8	8.6		

Names of Lessees	Names of Tenements	Names of Lives	Ages	Convent. Rents	Quay Dues	Heriot	Estimated net yearly value
Joseph Baker late Mark Noble	Hawke's House and Garden	John Huggill Thomas Huggill Betsy Huggill	44 3.7 25	2.0.	1.8.6 1.6	3.4	12.0.0
John Willing late Richd Edgcumbe	Warrens or Kerswills and Wardens 2 Houses & Garden Willing ...	Mary Quint Edgcombe Jno Thomas Edgcombe Jno Willing Junr	41 27 29	8.0	3.0	5.10	16.0.0 12.0.0
Joseph Baker	Sparkes 3 Dwellings and Small Shop	Joseph Baker Sarah his Wife Sarah their Daur	51 55 18	3.6	1.6	2.6	16.10.0
The Same	Pikes 3 Dwellings & Garden	Fanny Baker Ann Baker	14 16	2.3	1.6	3.4	14.0.0
George Kingston	Hooper's Good House Workshop Back Let Quay and Garden	George Kingston Jane his Wife Char H. Wayomouth	53 47 27	6.0	1.6	3.4	14.0.0
Henry Tomlinson	Warrens 2 Dwellings and Garden	Letth Stadon J. W. Tomlinson Mary Tomlinson	33 18 22	1.4	1.6	2.6	18.0.0
Charles M. Buckeel	Joints 3 Houses containing 12 Rooms at 5 G each	Chat Martin Couch Chat Martin Tood Caroline Tood	9 10 8	8.0	1.6	8.0	50.0.0
Mr Mould late Mary Blake	Part of Trustees House Orchard and Garden (admr Watsons) & Willis or property House ...	Ann Worthy Mary Blake J. G. Newbry	69 50 13	3.0	1.6	5.0	30.0.0 36.0.0
Thomas Oliver	Part of Do House Garden and Orchard	John Hawke	35	3.0	1.6	5.0	20.0.0
George Wyatt	the whole consist of 4 ... Rooms			13.6	2.2.0		
	consisting of Shop & 2 ... Rooms & ... 1 a Bakehouse ... worth at clear 17	John Hawke	33	3.0	1.6	5.0	27.0.0
	... for the other Part kept 4 Rooms & ... of garden worth clear 10						
outer Dunstone House &c higher Room							

These Hooe Barton Farm estate details are held in the Plymouth and West Devon Record Office, Plymouth. Accession No 121/4. Reproduced by kind permission.

COPELAND'S VISIT 1968

Mr. G. W. Copeland F.S.A. F.A.M.S. of Topsham was the highest authority on ancient buildings in the Plymouth area and in Devon generally was regarded as the best authority on ancient church and ecclesiastical architecture. He was invited to make a visit to the farm in 1968. This is his report to the The Old Plymouth Society.

West Hooe Farm or Westhoobury.
An old farmhouse, much altered, especially the West, but with some slight remains of a late medieval building: two ruined ends of a structure with thick walls, from which, towards the North, a dilapidated stone wall returns East to enclose formerly a court. In the remaining part of this East wall is a good granite doorway with a two centred head and apparently of the mid 15th century. It is continuously ogee and hollow-chamfer moulded with the remains of one jamb-stop, seemingly of cushion form.

Hooe Barton Farm at the time of G.W. Copeland's visit in 1968. For car buffs: A Hillman Minx is parked across. Outside Barton Shop is a 1.5 litre Riley.
Photo Stanley Goodman.
Collection of Esther Arnold.

In his **History of Plymouth and her Neighbours** Bracken states that a length of wall and an old arched doorway **are the remains of a chapel dedicated to St. Anne which formerly stood here.**

Licence to celebrate Divine Service in the Chapel was granted by Bishop Stafford of Exeter to John Brakler and his wife Thomasina in 1407. One authority states that a small chapel was probably built here in 1100 by permission of the Bishop of Exeter and that remains of the old house and chapel were to be seen as late as the middle of the 19th century. Lysons states that here was a chapel of St. Catherine mentioned in Bishop Stafford's Register in 1413.

The dimensions of the doorway question are: width between jambs 2' 9"; height to inner apex 7' 9".

Whatever the dedication, and that to St. Anne appears to be the correct one, there is no real evidence that this doorway has ever been elsewhere than where it now is, where it served as a subsidiary entrance through the wall enclosing the court before the house, It may have been the entrance to a small private Oratory pertaining to the house but even that is very doubtful. Any earlier chapel, such as that of 1100 must have stood elsewhere, unless it was completely rebuilt, as there is now no trace of such early work at West Hooe.

The north end of the house adjoins a large stone barn with a modern roof, transeptal projections east and west, narrow splayed slits and two large blocked openings high up at the east. The walls are slightly over 3 feet thick. The open timber roof has been restored with old crooked collar-beams. The lateral 'porches' near the centre are shallow, with a large rectangular recess with a wooden lintel in east wall of the south one.* The Barn makes a curious junction with the house.

The south and east of the house are an old dilapidated rectangular chimney-stack on the gable and a gabled projection respectively. South of this projection, in the angle with the East wall, is a similar but lower projection which contains a straight wooden staircase. There are no old windows or doorways visible or apparently surviving. The interior has in general been completely modernised, and has plain flat plaster ceilings and modern fireplaces. There is a fair 18th century main staircase at the rear of the small entrance-hall, with turned balusters, scrolled handrail and square newel posts, the middle one with a plain pendant.

It is possible that restoration, rather than complete demolition, might reveal some interesting, but still hidden minor features. If possible, the late medieval doorway and a part of the wall containing it, should be preserved. It would be highly desirable also if the barn could be preserved and adapted to some modern requirements.

* If Copeland is referring to the 'grease cupboard', and this is the only large square recess with a wooden lintel, then this should read 'in the South wall of the West one.' In any case there are only north and south walls to the east and west porches.

Though he could never be accused of painting a detailed textual picture his somewhat basic observations did lend authoritative weight to the gathering campaign to save the Barn and have it listed.

Around this time there was considerable conjecture regarding the name of the chapel. St. Anne's was favoured by some because it gave weight to the theory that it was the origin of the name Turnchapel. Whilst attractive this is also suspect on the grounds that it was some distance over a hill from Turnchapel and even some way removed by boat, the source of a place name being usually geographically very close to, or prominent in some way, in relation to the location.

Ivy Langdon, who was then secretary of the Plymstock and District Civic Society and researching material for her excellent book 'The Plymstock Connection' wrote to Stanley Goodman (secretary of The Old Plymouth Society) to thank him for the copy of Copeland's report and went on to say:

"I have come to the conclusion that the reference to the Chapel of St. Catherine in Lysons, which may have been taken from Leland, is incorrect, and that this really refers to the Chapel of St. Catherine which was formerly on the Hoe at Plymouth. You may be interested to know that Oliver's Monasticon refers to a licence granted on August 4th, 1337, to John de Englebourne, Prior of Plympton to celebrate divine service in St. Laurence's Chapel, " infra manerium de Westhoo," in Plymstock parish. I can find no mention of St. Anne's Chapel although I feel this name is clearly associated with Turnchapel, formerly Tan Chapel."

There is a slight discrepancy here. In the letter she refers to the license being granted in 1337. In her subsequent book she gives the date as 1387. Having not had the opportunity to read the original monasticon I am unable to say which is correct.

The west side of the farmyard. The main gate has been taken away and a pile of chippings covers the position of the apple crusher. The builders are using the farmyard as an access road. Drainage pipes are stacked alongside one of the sheds. The MoD pumping station remains to the right. Photograph by Stanley Goodman, 1968.

The farm buildings seen from the site of Pollard Close. Photograph by Stanley Goodman, 1968. Collection Sheila Coleman.

FARM RECOLLECTIONS

ROY HOPPER

Roy started work in Hooe Barton Farm immediately after leaving Plymstock School in 1950, when he was 15.

Minneapolis-Moline Tractor

"I used to start by doing the milk round with the girls, Jean and Cynthia. We had a big Austin. It had a flat boot lid that we used to drop down to put the churns on and carry around. That was Jack's transport! Before that I think Ernie Sherrell had a horse and cart but that was before my time. I drove around then stayed back on the farm to do any ploughing or other work. I passed my test on the tractor and bought one of my own. In the end I had collected quite a bit of gear, a pick-up baler, a plough, grass machine, tractors... I did a little bit of contracting to other farmers but it wasn't too good. Farmers were very poor payers "Pay you next week, boy!" and it would go on like that. I felt I was doing it more like a hobby. I used to go out to Cundy's, which was to the right of where the ski slope is now [Leigham area]. That's where I learned to drive a combine harvester. That was an experience!

We were working on Outer Hill at the top of Staddiscombe at the time. The chap who was driving the combine came from Ivybridge and he used to like playing darts. So as it was a Friday evening he wanted to get off so he asked if I could finish off the field. So I said I'd have a go. He said "There's only one thing to remember, don't turn the machine with the bags on the downhill side." They were baggers in those days, stored the grain in sacks on the side. Well I was dead chuffed, sitting up there driving this machine and it was getting dark and what did I do? Turned the wrong way! Well the whole thing tipped up and stayed leaning over for what seemed ages. Came back down eventually but that gave me a turn I can tell you! Come the end I was using my own tractor to do Jack's work because his old Fordson was a bit over the hill.

You had some characters used to come here contracting. Henry Lugar, he used to do a lot of contracting. Mr Baker, up at Staddiscombe, 'Squeaker' we used to call him 'cause he had a little squeaky voice. Rough Doddridge, he drove a huge tractor. An MM, a Minneapolis-Moline. He *was* a big feller, that was some machine. He came down the road and swung

into Jack's yard with the threshing unit and the baler all hitched up to the tractor in a line. We used to put the corn ricks in the farmyard, just in from the gate. We used to do all the threshing there.

The farmhouse was a long building, panelled inside. The only toilet was outside. As you went in the door you had a hallway and on the left was a big black trestle [settle?]. In line with the front door on the right there was another room to the right, a fair sized room, then you turned left into the big room where a big fire used to be at the back and from there you went out the passageway. Before you hit the kitchen on the left hand side there was a set of stairs to go up to the top. They ran up the back of the house, you could see the back garden from the windows up the stairs. Upstairs was just one long narrow passageway with all the bedrooms in the front. There was Winnie's mother and father there too but her dad died soon after I started work. Jack had come from Ugborough to run Hooe Barton farm. He had a younger brother who ran a farm out at Smithaleigh behind Sparkwell.

That shippon on the east side was always known as Palace Court*. We used it for birthing calves. Many's the calf I've pulled out in there!

The shippon on the west side we used for milking. You can still see the stalls and the grips in the concrete for the cows hooves. Of course it was hand milk-

Inside the West Shippon. Feb. 2000.

ing and the whole of the inside of the Shippon was cement rendered in 1950 because of Tuberculosis (TT) regulations. I think it was done by H. Hockin, he was a local plumber/builder. Or was the chap who actually did it called Steve something or other? He was Australian, stationed at Mount Batten with the Australian Air Force. You know... he married Joan Luscombe from Hooe. After the war he worked for Mr. Hockin, he was a local builder.

The farm supplied all the milk for the area. I used to drive this old Austin and take the milk girls around; we put the churns on the drop-down boot lid.

The barn was just used for storage come the end. Mangols for cows and that. The farm used to supply not only the milk but the vegetables too for quite an area around. Did good business they did. I think they supplied milk to Savery's ice cream parlour which was over where the new houses are on the site of the old Mountbatten Social Club; called Harris Close now.

Jack and Winnie Ford were lovely people. Jack used to keep Greyhounds, a sort of sporting hobby as well as bringing them on and training them for people and tracks like Pennycross Stadium in Plymouth. He had up to six at one time. I looked after them mostly and took them up the fields to run them and train them starting and that as well as doing my farm work. About three times a week we used to go to our dog running. Jack was in with a group of people who were interested in greyhound racing. Lot of money seemed to change hands but not much of it stuck to me! There was Fred Osborne, he was a Plymouth bookmaker, Bill Phipps who worked for him,

Photograph collection of Roy Hopper

Roy Hopper in 1950 with L to R: Turner's Bridge (Named after Winnie Ford's Mother), Judy (who ended up as a pet), Roy's Pal and Nancy's Gift.

Jack Herd, a Plymouth Butcher, Bert Carter, who owned Exeter Greyhound Track and a Torquay bookie called Bernard Redfern. I remember him coming to the farm with his daughter, who was quite young then about 12, 13 I suppose. They were going on up to the point to point racing at Buckfastleigh. A pretty little thing she was with very striking chestnut ginger coloured hair, her father had the same colour. She was called Anthea...**

The black brindle dog in the picture is named after me, called Roy's Pal. A good dog too, running weight sixty-six and a half pounds. Used to run wide and favoured trap six on the outside.

There was a big well in the field just behind the farm, in what is some gardens in Bear Close now. About 18 to 20 feet deep, you needed your ladder to get down into it. That fed water to the milk cooler outside the dairy. It was a square tank, brick I think. The walls came up about a meter above ground level and we put concrete slabs over the top. It was also fed in part from the reservoir [Bayly's] higher up the Brakes tucked up in the corner. What there was up there were two sets of red building brick cattle troughs with ball cocks on and to the right of them was another one but he was covered over and sunk down in the ground. They were all in a line like one two three. As you go up to that corner with the little gate that's still in the bottom, that's were he is. They were fed from clay pipe land drains and also drained down in clay pipes. We used to have a lot of trouble with tree roots breaking into the delivery pipes and we'd have to rod them out to clear them or else the troughs would overflow.

The water from the big reservoir fed the milk cooler in the dairy of the farm then ran on out to join the spring that flowed past the corner by the farm gate and into the lake.

Now there was another spring that came out into the Lake where the pumping station is now. It flowed out of the wall just up the hill from what is now Harris Gardens. There was a small archway like in the wall and the water flowed all the time, overflowing down a pipe and into the Lake.

Shute quay was the biggest supply though. When the water entered the top farm garden the culvert was open to the air, we used to use sluices to divert the water into the garden. When it got to the lower garden it dipped so it must have gone underground to Shute Quay. Never dried up that. I've seen ducklings go down that stream where it was open back in the farm gardens and get carried away down the culvert to reappear unharmed out at Shute Quay. The left hand tap in the wall at Shute Quay had a bracket above the tap so buckets could be hung on this while being filled.

That American Army grease? Well you know the shippons up the west side: First there was where the car used to go, then Tapley's then a store shed, by the door. That shed was full of it. They were brown drums about two feet high by a foot in diameter, all covered with American serial numbers. There was two lots. One was like pure vaseline, that was for packing bearings and the other was high melting point. We used a lot of it, so did Chris Willdern who had the Garage. That came in the night I think, goodness knows where from. Hooe was very silent but little mice worked at night!

Bayly's had a timber yard at the entrance to Hooe Lake and they used to season the timber in rafts floating in the lake. 14 x 14in [355 x 355mm], 18 x 18in [457 x 457mm] and 2ft x 2ft [610 x 610mm], by anything up to 40ft [12.2metres] long. They were for sleepers and telephone poles mainly. I worked the last telegraph pole on the dockside over there. They had a skinning machine over there [to take the bark off] and by God if they got damp in the cargo you couldn't do nothing with them, very difficult. They was deadly machines.

I remember as a young boy playing cricket around the back of Broomfield/Fanshaw Way, what is now the council estate. This would be 1944, a Saturday afternoon. Just a knock about, I was playing with Tom Savery, who later became Mayor, when there was an almighty noise from the top of Hooe Hill. It was the rocket battery doing a test firing, but they didn't tell anyone and all these [anti-aircraft] rockets went up in a square group. We all fell flat on our faces. Thought the end had come!"

*A name that links back to the days when Hooe Barton farm was a substantial trading place. On maps circa 1901 the area to the east of the barn, between it and Shute Quay, was named Palace Court.

** From 1971-77 Anthea Redfern was co-presenter on the TV Game Show 'The Generation Game' with Bruce Forsyth, whom she married. As she had a new dress each programme Bruce would invite her to show  it off with the phrase "Give us a twirl Anthea..."

Hooe Barton Farm in 1968. The three shippons referred to by Roy Hopper are on the left front. The west shippon used for milking is the stone built one with a door, next to the arch and farmhouse. The lean-to shippons housed (L to R) Jack Ford's Austin Car for milk delivery, George Tapley's workshop and a store that at one time held a lot of American grease. Original Photographs by Stanley Goodman.

JEAN PARSONS (NEE CRAVEN)

Jean Craven worked in The Lake Stores after leaving school then became one of the farm milk girls with Cynthia Gwilliam (nee Williams).

"My dad was from Cheshire and my mother Suffolk. I was born in Shoeburyness and came here when I was eighteen months. We lived where St. Lukes' Hospice is now. My dad was in the army and they were married quarters for the army at Stamford Fort and I lived in Staddon Fort for a little while. Then we went to live in Bovisand, there were married quarters on the right as you go down to the Fort. Not the white painted house, the stone ones. Of course I used to be on the beach all day.

When he came out of the Army we were looking for somewhere to live and he was on the pipeline at Radford. I remember that because they were nearly all Irish working on that.

When my dad died and mum was quite old she went to live in the same house as she had been in all those years ago when first married, the married quarters for Staddon Fort that the Hospice have now. Full circle!

I left school in the Christmas 1943 when I was 15 and went to work in January 1944 at The Lake Stores though we just called it Mahons. It was run by Mr and Mrs Mahon then. They all used to sleep in there, Mr and Mrs and their two children. I wasn't there very long, about six months, I didn't like it. I remember all the Americans down there, they were working on Barton Road and they widened Hooe Road all the way from Radford Dip to Belle View, well it was just like a lane before then. Built a beautiful wall all along the left hand side, about 5ft high all made of Devon stone. That all went when they built the houses off Reddicliff Road. [The road was being widened so they could get their vehicles and equipment through for embarkation at Sycamore Beach, Turnchapel.] I don't remember too much about the Americans, my Dad used to keep us away from them!

Working on the farm was nice. I started there around June 1944 as a milk girl. Plenty of lovely fresh air

and the food was wonderful. They had their own spotlessly clean dairy, opposite the house. All stone it was, very cold in there. They made their own butter and I learned how to use the wooden butter pats to make up blocks, they had a rose pattern on them. They made their own cream. Then there were churns for the milk, you either had a measure or a bottle.

Beside the dairy they used to sell vegetables. Potatoes, cabbage all things like that. I can see the gates now into the farmyard. Big double gates. We used to use this Austin Seven with a board, a big board put on the back of it to hold the churns. And you'd have the measures and the bottle inside. And we used to cart that around everyday. I think we supplied just about everybody in Hooe and Turnchapel, Homer Park, up Hexton Hill. I used to go down at six in the morning to start. Mrs Ford used to get most of it packed, we used to start up at St. Anne's. I liked everyone we used to visit. We used to take eggs too.

In the farmhouse it was all gas lighting. There was a big settle on the right going in. They used to feed us too in the kitchen. Mrs Ford used to have her mother there and she used to cook the breakfast for us coming back from the morning round. Lovely food All this fresh bacon, lovely everyday.

I never liked going down in the Barn though, I didn't like the cows very much. They kick out you know. They used to milk in that little shippon. The Barn was used mainly for storage, hay and that. They kept turkeys too and chickens. He used to kill them off at Christmas, feathers everywhere. They chase you turkeys do so I was always very careful when I went for a walk up through the field where the turkeys were. They were free range, just roamed

Jean Craven in 1945.

around. We used to go up there sometimes to fetch the cows down, I didn't like that very much, Cynthia liked that job better than I did.

Where those houses are built, Pollard Close and all that, it was a huge field. I can remember the hay making used to go on up there. My dad and brother used to help with the hay making, they had quite a few men at hay making time. All horses drawing rakes and things. Real old fashioned!

Arscott Lane at the time so I had to get back up there. I had a few bruises after that day.

For entertainment we used to go dancing at Down Thomas, used to walk there. Used to walk up over Hexton Hill and around Staddiscombe, that way. Used to walk everywhere in those days. Well there was nothing around here. You know they say there's not a lot to do around here now? Well we didn't have a lot to do either but we used to manage.

Hay making at Hooe Barton Farm circa 1940. Bill Dunn is on the hay rake
Photograph courtesy of Alf Salmon.

There was a kitchen garden at the back of the farmhouse. He had strawberries in there. He kept bees too. I remember him in the hat and veil though I can't remember him getting much honey. He tried his hand at just about anything.

I worked there quite a few years. I left to get married in 1951. I remember Mrs Ford came to fetch me from Flete Nursing home after I'd had my son, Keith. She came in that little Austin they used for the milk. Very kind they were. They were very good to me, well to everyone who worked for them really.

We had drifting snow in 1947, terrible winter that was, and we had to go delivering the milk. We got up the top of Church Hill there and really got stuck. So my boss, Jack Ford, says "Well we've got to get down to Turnchapel somehow maid." So we left the car and carried a churn and some bottles and we got down to Turnchapel on our backsides more or less. And they said "You're late today!" and I had fallen down about six times and I was really fed up. I couldn't have got home till late that day because we had to deliver to all of them or nearly all of them. We had a big round, just about everyone had milk from us. The snow was really deep in the lanes like St. John's Drive and Amacre Drive. I was living at

Mind you I never had a weekend off and used to work Sundays too down there. And Christmas. I used to like Christmas day because they used to give you a mince pie and all that sort of thing and I looked forward to the tips. Cynthia and I used to count out the tips and Mr. Ford would say, joking like, "Hey, half of that's mine!" and I'd say "No, you don't get any, we delivered it!" Our wages were £2 a week.

When we lived up Arscott Lane my dad used to pick lovely watercress in the fields where Reddicliff houses are now.

Mr Tapley used to have his monumental place. Before you went through the double gates he had a display on the grass there. He had a monkey there. One of the airmen from Mount Batten, Tommy Bowker, used to pinch the monkey every Saturday night, after a few drinks, and take it back Sunday morning. Heavy it was too, a good 28 lbs (about 13 kilos). Used to say "I've got to get up early Sunday and take Mr Tapley's monkey back". Early 1950's that was. Did that regular as clockwork and took it back without fail. George, my husband, was in the airforce. We girls got to know them all. When the [Australian] Air Force came we were alright for dancing partners."

CYNTHIA GWILLIAM (NEE WILLIAMS)

Cynthia was born at 3 Croft Terrace, Hooe, in 1934, one of eight children. She worked with Jean Craven in the Dairy of Hooe Barton Farm immediately after leaving Plymstock Secondary School in 1949, aged 15. Cynthia left the Farm in 1954 to work in Woolworth's in Plymouth. After she was married she went to Cyprus with her husband who was in the RAF.

"I was on the dairy side of the farm, you see, the milk girl. Jean was the other girl I worked with. We used to go round with the milk with churns on the back of a van, with a tap, You knyw? That's how we used to do. itPut a quart of milk in like a tin can and then you'd take it in. Mr Ford used to drive with Jean and I. We used to do all up Westway, all up over the hill, Mountbatten, Turnchapel and practically all Hooe. 'Course it was a lot smaller then you see.[Not so many houses]. Our till, well we used to have a bag, I mean they knew we was as honest as anything, Jean and I, and what [Mrs Ford] used to do was just put a float in our bag, she wouldn't know how much she put in there but she knew we wouldn't take a ha'penny. That was our money bag to go around. Some paid everyday and some paid weekly you see, and there was some naughty ones that we used to have to knock on the door first!

The dairy part was behind the outbuilding in the front, it was in the inner part, opposite the Farm-house. There was a cooler there, a big steel thing with water running through it. We also had a big vegetables round, of a Friday, so they must have grown vegetables. I remember being in the dairy at that time [1949] butter, margarine and lard was on ration, I remember doing that up and putting it in bags. The butter and lard was bought in. If I re-member rightly our butter ration was 2ozs [57grams] a week, margarine was 4ozs [114grams] a week and lard was 4ozs a week. I'm sure that's right. We used to get the butter and margarine in half pound blocks, as we do now, and we had to cut it up into two and four ounce pieces, wrap it in a piece of greaseproof and put it in a paper bag and mark the name of the customer on it. I think the lard was in a big slab and we had to measure it on the scales. We started early, about seven o'clock, and we'd do the first round. Then we went back to the farm and have a lovely big fry-up breakfast. She was a wonderful cook, Mrs Ford, we used to have lunch there too. We finished at four. I think I did every other Sunday too. You know, Jean and I would share the Sundays.

You went into the door [of the farmhouse] inside in the Hall was a big settle. There was a lounge on the left, she had a beautiful leather suite in there but I don't know what ornaments she had. There was a passageway running out to the back where we used to eat in the kitchen. They also had granny and grandad, they used to live there. Mrs Fords mother and father, dear old souls! There was all bedrooms upstairs. I didn't see much of the rest of the house.

We started with the churns on the back of the black car. We had to keep it all spotless, scrubbing it down like. All the churns and the bottles. All the Dairy, well you had to. Later some milk was bottled as well as some sold from churns.

We used to look forward to Christmas because of the tips. We used to get half a crown sometimes [22.5p] and that was won-derful, well it was a lot of money then, we used to be thrilled. A lot used to call me 'Smiler' because I was always laughing, I was always a happy sort you know?

The Barn was just used for storage, hay and straw piled up in there. There was a little shop [by the garage], my grandad used to go over there. I've for-gotten the name of who ran it when I was a little girl but we used to call him 'Uncle Arkie'. [Hercules Doddridge]. Dear old man. Frank Rogers had the garage and the paper shop after him.

They had a garden at the back of the house. I don't remember much about that but they used to grow flowers and vegetables there I think.

The farmyard was cobbled or stone, the inner one was slabs. There was a big circular trough by the gate by Westway. The cows used to drink out of it. That disappeared soon after the place was sold.

Mr and Mrs Ford retired when the farm was sold. They never had no children."

ROGER WESTLAKE

Roger Westlake owns Staddon Heights Farm, which has been in his family for over 100yrs. His land borders the fields that belonged to Hooe Barton Farm and runs down the north face of the Brakes.

"When Edna Sherrell sold Hooe Barton Farm to Wimpey it was when Plymouth City Council took over this area from Devon CC. The day before they took it over Wimpey put a bulldozer in to push down the Jennycliff Lane fence so they could say work had begun, otherwise they might not have been able to go ahead with the development because Plymouth were against it.

Jack and Winnie Ford retired to Ivybridge and we took over the land that was left after the sale to Wimpey. About the early 80's I bought the remaining land from Edna Sherrell.

The water pipe on the map that runs from Fort Staddon to Fort Stamford? All the surface water from Fort Staddon went into a sand and gravel filter in the moat. Probably still does. That was then piped down to Fort Stamford and I believe it also supplied water to the churchyard. Wimpey broke the pipe somewhere in Lalebrick Road when they were building the houses.

The top reservoir collected the water from the valley coming down the Brakes. It was connected to a pattern of land drain pipes up the valley, we've dug them up in various places, and the water that was collected went to Shute Quay and may have gone on to Bayly's timber yard at the entrance to Hooe Lake but I wouldn't know if it was piped over there or how it got there.

The reservoir was fenced around with a concrete posts and chain link fence. The last time I went down there to the back of these houses the fence had gone and there were cabbages growing in there.

The big ditch dug across the back of the end houses was put in by Wimpey to try and stop the water coming down into the houses. They piped it through a 12 inch main. The inspection pit for the old reservoir is right in the corner of the last house in Lalebrick Road.

The next reservoir down was a big well, one you could walk in with steps down. A square building with a door. It was out in the field. They used that field to grow kale and fodder for their cows. It was a very old well, supplied water for the farm, it went to their dairy and milk cooler. Well 'Rough' filled that in. 'Rough' Dodderidge used to drive a 955 machine for Wimpey. We'd known 'Rough' for years because he was an agricultural contractor and used to come here with the thresher. After the war he worked for Lacey's at Newton Ferrers. We lost track of 'Rough' when threshers went out but all of a sudden 'Rough' appears on the scene and he was driving for Wimpey. He was down there helping build the houses. He was deformed in his neck. He always carried his head on one side, couldn't straighten his head. Mad as a hatter he was. We called him 'Rough' because he was a bit rough with the machines like! If there was a bank or hill and he thought a machine could go up there then he would try. Like a challenge to him it was.

There's a main underground electric cable running right up the centre of the valley which is the supply to the Staddon Fort. When we cleaned the valley out a bit, in the 1980's I suppose, we were down there ploughing and I went down the see how the chap was getting on and he said he was hooked up on something like the root of a tree and was going to see if he could cut it away with a hammer and cold chisel. I said it didn't look like the root of a tree and we cleaned him off and it was that electric cable. SWEB tried to say that we had stripped soil off because the cable was now so close to the surface and should have been more than four foot down. However when they went further along the line and put a shovel in they hit the protection brick immediately. "Oh Dear" he says. They got a team in to rebury it and found that it was five feet down at the bottom but just under the turf near the top. Originally it went straight up through the farmyard from the main gate but now it comes off the substation in Beare Close.

Jack Ford got injured by a concrete block that fell on him. He was out threshing at the time and they had been using concrete blocks to hold sheets of galvanised on top of the rick. A block slid off the top of a rick and hit him on the shoulder. After that he had a job to use one arm. When that was I don't know but after that Winnie used to do a lot of the work.

It was always Winnie who walked up to fetch the cows. I can see her now walking up through the little path that used to go up by nursery field, there was a track that came up by that. Sometimes she would wear a plain coat or a blue gabardine mac with a headscarf and the cows always seemed to be at the top of the hill, you know?

I went down to help them with their farm sale. They were getting on then and although they had agreed to retire I suppose it all come as a bit of a shock to them and they didn't really want to do it. I helped sort everything out, walked the cows around the ring at the sale. There had been a monumental mason in one of the sheds against the Barn. He had retired some time before. When we opened up one of these sheds there were all these tins of grease. I says to Jack Ford "Here what's all this then?" "Oh," he says "that was left behind by the Americans during the war. That's grease that stays pliable in freezing weather." It was in tins about 15 by 30 cms. He said I could have it so we brought it up here. It's all gone now of course. They went to live in Ivybridge then. They had come from farming at Ugborough and came down to run this one.

They were alright. Winnie always amused me when they were pulling mangols and putting them into the Barn. Winnie knew how many mangols were in that Barn and she knew how many she could feed her cows each day for the number of days they thought the winter would be so that they came out at the right amount for what they had. Nobody else would have thought like that. If a cow needed eight a day it got eight a day and if you ran out you went onto something else. They had South Devon Reds to start with then Friesians come the end.

South Devon Cow. Similar to those owned by Ernie Sherrell. They are a dark reddish brown.

Ernie and George Sherrell had the foot and mouth disease on the farm in the early thirties. The cows were buried down in what is now Pollard Close. The owner of the cattle got compensation for each cow, which in those days would have been about eight pounds a cow. Ernie would have had a herd of about twenty cows. No farmer would have had very many in those days. He would have got about £160 but that was it, you didn't get anything for consequential loss for the milk sales that had gone *and* the

farm has to stay empty for six months before you can restock. I remember my grandad saying that it cost him a fortune and that Ernie and George were, in a way, better off because grandad had to keep all his cattle in and it was spring and they had to buy in fodder for them. In the end they were importing hay from Norway, cost them a fortune.

Eventually the milk business came back after a couple of years or so. Then they had to sell direct to the milk companies rather than working a milk round themselves.

Grandad Shepherd, that's my mother's father, used to milk cows behind the Royal Oak; he rented the land behind there and his parents had the Royal Oak. Of course the stables were there too, what is now the pub beer garden.

If you look at the Brakes from the bottom, to the left of the valley, all that scrub was fruit gardens in the thirties. There were strawberries, black currants and raspberries. When mother was a little girl she used to go up there in a pony and trap and take tea

up to those that were working up there. Harry Burridge used to go up there quite recently, almost until he died. He knew where the remaining bushes were and he used to pick black currants and that. If you look you can see its still mainly scrub, there are only young trees."

East side of the Brakes above the Barn. 2001. An area that contained fruit bushes in the 1930's.

ALF SALMON

the pipes are still there to take away the water from the road, though its not making a very good job of it at the present time.

Alf was Hooe's oldest resident. He died on 23rd March 2001 having just turned 98.
He worked on the Turnchapel ferry boats on leaving school at 14, and then in the fertiliser chemical works at Cattedown for 16 years before joining the GPO as a telephone engineer 'joiner and plumber' on underground cables. He lived in his house in Barton Road since 1928.

"The first farmer I remember, he was called Hine. After he left Mr Sherrell took over and then Mr Ford took over after that and that were the end.

It was a dairy farm then and sold milk and used to deliver it as well.

Seen quite a few changes here, really. Used to be able to look over across here [the top of the Lake] and see the Tea Gardens across there. All the children used to come along, sit down and have their teas.; church outings and one thing and another, used to have their tea party right across there where the new houses are. [Harris Court]. There was a market garden there, he had a milk round as well, people called Harris then, they had a building at the back of the house and they had a big orchard at the back.

The houses at Westway were built just after I came here.

That big house up here, St. Annes' House [approaching Jennycliff] that used to be the vicarage when I was a boy. The vicar used to have a path from the church to the house, through the fields like. There used to be a swing gate 'side the field so he could get through alright.

Down near where my front gate is now, that used to be the main gate into the fields here that the houses are built on. Right across the opposite side [of the main road] was the main gate to the farm. On [the site of] that first house here there used to be watercress, used to pick all our watercress there once upon a time. They built over that and the people who lived there first had a lot of trouble with water coming up but I think they must have got rid of that alright. The spring's still there and though its buried now

What remains of the entrance to the farmyard, March 2001. It is now the access road to the car park behind the precinct development. The driveway immediately to the right, between the old farm entrance and the first house is the road to the oil fuel pumping station that was situated in the clear land in the centre of the picture.

The water from the hills used to come down to what they call Shute Quay over there. Many years ago a couple of ladies round here used to keep pigs. They'd have a pig's belly as they called it, and wash it out over there at Shute Quay. Used to do all their washing there.

George Tapley had a monumental mason's works on the side of the barn. His daughter's still living around here somewhere. He was born in that house next to the Post Office. Very old that house.

In the war this was, I went down to shut the front gate and I heard a lot of moaning down there and I wondered what had happened and I went across on the side, before there was any building at all, and there was a chap kicking another one, I think he would have kicked him to death if I hadn't come along. Before I knew anything I was on the floor as well. I came in and the wife said "What's happened to you?" as I was all bruised up. "I went to somebody's aid", I said, "never no more!" But wouldn't have minded, I could have defended myself but it was all unexpected. I was in my slippers like, I was just going to bed. I never knew what the quarrel was and the boy that was being kicked lived a little way up here but he never came down to apologise for what I went through, but that's all in the past.

There was two houses over there on the other side [of the lake] one of them was blown up in the war. Gentleman called Burgoyne used to grow garden plants. His son took it over. They had an air raid one night that demolished the house with the wife, two women and two children inside. The men were outside walking about like and the house collapsed just like that. That's just on the right as you turn up for Hexton.

The person that had the garage built was a person called Doddridge. He had the place built for himself and had the garage built as a garage only. He was a relative of Sheila Coleman. His son took it over after him but he couldn't get on with it so he sold it to Frank Rogers.

Frank Rogers used to have a farm. In the woods, you know there's a big house in the woods? That used to be Rogers' farm. In the middle of the woods there; a farmer called Pursey had it, then, when he left, Rogers took it over. You know where you go down over Radford hill, the dip? Where the tanks are at the present time? There used to be a path there right up to the woods. In between there and Staddiscombe used to be the farm, that's where Rogers had his farm. Still there now. [Barn farm]. After I retired I went up and did a couple of jobs on his roof, slates, well lead more or less. You can get to it by going up to Higher Hooe and turn right towards The Retreat [along Belle View Road] keep left and go down into the woods [Arscott Lane]. There used to be a path all the way to Staddiscombe. [The path still exists and is marked on current maps]. The road went up to the farm, that's as far as it went. A little way before the farm there's a path leading off to the right. Goes across two or three fields up into Staddiscombe.

Rogers he didn't start the paper round. His mother started the paper round. His mother used to do that, her was a widow and had a corrugated iron bungalow this end of Staddiscombe. There used to be a bakery there and on this side of the road there used to seven or eight steps to the end of the path and on the right hand side was this bungalow of hers. Mrs Rogers used to do the papers in there I suppose. Her husband died and she had a family of three or four I think. She used to do the paper round and when she stopped her eldest son took over and when he went, joined the Police Force or something, Frank Rogers took over.

The farm here was dairy mainly. All the water they used came from the hills for washing their cans and one thing and another. There used to be a reservoir up the top, on the Brakes there as I call it. Just at the bottom of the Brakes here. You used to get an orchard between the farm and a market garden that used to be between the two like. A bomb dropped there during the war they had to do a lot of clearing up.

The man who kept the market garden when I was a boy was called Fletcher. He used to do all the vegetables like.

[Roy Hopper] was working over the farm when I used to go over to help Jack Ford the farmer. Roy was working there then as a boy like you know. I was just messing around, helping like. Getting the cows in, tying them up and one thing and another, helping to feed them. Wasn't paid work, just done it voluntary. They were Devon cows, all reddish brown. I don't think he had any others. When Mr Sherrell was there he had to lose 20 cattle with foot and mouth. They burnt them up there. [Indicating the West side of the Brakes]

Yes I went in the farmhouse, all the floor was stone. The stairway was very narrow and the ceilings were very low. The house was attached to the barn. You'd go through the arch and on the left hand side was the entrance to the farmhouse, go in and the kitchen was on your left."

Remains of the front living room fireplace in the south wall of the Barn. March 2001.

EDDIE RENDLE

Eddie Rendle was 70 when interviewed on February 3rd. He had worked mainly for Sid Phillips, who had the farm in Radford Dip.

There were troops at the farm 1939/40. They were under canvas at the back of the farm, Had some tin huts too. Supposed to have been guarding the oil tanks at Radford and Turnchapel.

"When Wimpey came in to build the tanks at Radford Depot in 1939 I used to ride a carrier bicycle from the Hooe Barton farm dairy up to Radford with a Primrose Dairy cardboard butter box in the carrier filled with cigarettes, chocolates, cartons of milks, eggs, etc. I also used to sit outside Mrs Hine's front door [in Hooe Road] and the Irish labourers used to buy off me what they wanted. I used to do a paper round for Frank Rogers, all up Underlane, out to Staddiscombe, Down Thomas and out to Langdon Court and Gabber. Used to take from seven in the morning to midday.

My dad was the chauffeur for Colonel Coates at the Manor [Belle View]. He did other things too, used to cut the croquet lawn in front of the house, like a billiard table it was. The Coates moved to Axminster and the house was stood empty. My father still had the cottage in Arscott Lane and he worked down on the tanks at Radford oil depot as a watchman.

My sister worked down at the farm with Mr. Sherrell and when he died with Mr Ford. Then she left and joined the WAAF as a cook. My brother Herbie, he's three year younger than me, he was down there for a short time. I worked for Sid Phillips down at his farm [bottom of Radford dip] I don't think anyone would do now what we did then. We used to work from six in the morning to six in the evening seven days a week. Hand milk cows twice a day. Clean the shippons, clean the churns. We didn't have a cooler, we used to stand the churns out in the stream. Then we'd go out on one round, come back at half past twelve, have bit of dinner, back down the farm again, get the cows in, milk them then go out on another round. 1939 that was, and nine bob [45p] a week!

I knew Harry Burridge who was the farm labourer down at Ford's farm for years. We were going to Choir Practice, I was in the church choir, I must have been, about what, eight, nine. They used to have trouble with stoats. The cows were in the field behind the elm trees where the houses in Westway are now. The stoats would get in there and they would suck a cow dry. And I always remember it as plain as day, we were standing by the gate, that's the one by Hooe Road, opposite Barton Road, and Harry Burridge saw this stoat coming down the field and as soon as it came out by the gate he stamped on it.

Jack Ford was almost bald and used to wear a cap all the time and gaiters with riding breeches. Winnie, his wife, was very upright, with glasses.

There was trees all up the side of the road to Jennycliff Road. Great big Elm trees, massive they were. Then Charlie Rowse bought that ground and built all those houses up Westways. In the field where the white bungalows are now, the naval houses that were, the land belonged to Stamford fort [MoD] and there were all hurdles in there for horse training and you used to see the artillery come out from Stamford fort and going over these jumps in the morning.

On the end of Stamford fort, this end, there is a big bank? Well most of that came out of the excavations for the naval bungalows. It wasn't like that before and right on the edge of the fort was the blacksmith's shop for shoeing the army horses. We used to go up and watch them. Mr. Craven did that, Jimmy Craven's father that was.

I remember there was that famous comedian, **Claude Dampier.** He stayed in a caravan behind Hooe Barton farm, big white thing it was. I think he was at the Palace Theatre. Summer it was and he was here for quite some time, about a month I think."

JUNE WHYTE

June has been totally involved with all aspects of local history for many years. Her knowledge of local matters is immense and she is a modest and generous benefactor.

"In November 1920 Ernest Sherrell bought Hooe Farm. The mortgage was discharged in November 1926 probably helped by selling Homer Hamacre field, No.400, to my great-uncle Clare Elford and Plot No.326 (currently the football field at Jennycliff) to Mrs E. A. Coates (see map on page 21).

My grandfather started building on what is called Church Hill now. Behind the first row of houses was the carpenter's workshop where Will Hine made all doors, window frames, skirtings etc. by hand using moulding planes and a manual mortice machine. Will was very patient with a five year old who wanted to use his tools and he taught me all I know about carpentry. Next to the workshop an old Pickford's van housed cement and other materials. A large pit contained lime (rather like a vanilla blancmange but much more lethal). Every concrete block was hand-made in a wooden framed machine by dropping in a wooden pallet, filling with concrete and raising the 'wafer' by lever and removing each one to set.

The cows still grazed in the rest of the field and when I went up for lessons, grandpa's parrot would travel on my shoulder and sit on the piles of timber to wait. She would imitate Sharp, the farm dog, and then all the cows would

gather around us for milking!
Every house had fires lit every day to dry out for 6 months before selling. When completed, each house in turn would be used as a workplace to glaze windows as Will finished them — I became an adept putty hand.

My grandparents moved into No.1 Church Hill and we occupied No.2 named Longstone and Hurlditch respectively after the Elford residences on Dartmoor.

There was a line of large oak trees where Westway is now, called the Twelve Apostles, these were removed when a builder [Rowse] acquired the land.

Between the top of Westway and Pollard Close a huge pit was dug to dispose of the animals during a period of foot and mouth disease in the thirties. The sound of a shot, then another carcass would be dragged across from the Barn to be burnt. The smell seemed to last for weeks. During this time, anyone entering or leaving the farmyard would have to step into a galvanised bath of disinfectant

As a small child it seemed a long walk to the farmhouse from No.2 to fetch milk and cream and I remember knocking on the door and Mrs Sherrell would take me across to the dairy to skim cream off the large scalding pans. I would also stop to watch our next door neighbour, George Tapley, at work in his stonemasons yard near the farm entrance.

Tales of the Barn fascinated me and I would sit in the den which Billy Tapley, Jackie Finch and I had built in one of the elm trees in Barton Road and dream of old galleons landing to store their loot in the Barn after long voyages and refill their water casks at Shute Quay.

Before English China Clay's work silted up the area, the Cattewater and Hooe Lake would have been much deeper. An old man from Turnchapel told me that, before Plymouth Breakwater was built, there would be as many as 20 ships sheltering in the Lake during storms."

THE LAKE STORES   BARBARA MAHON

1931. Mrs Winifred Tapper leases the land next to Shute Quay from Hooe Barton Farm owner Ernest Sherrell and employs Crocker's Builders of Goosewell to erect a shop and living accommodation. The Lake Stores is built but called 'Harwin' after Harry and Winifred Tapper. The Tappers buy the freehold in 1933. They run the shop until March 1939 when they move to Oreston and lease the shop to Josephine and Stephen Mahon. The Mahons run the shop, calling it 'The Lake Stores' until 1951 when they leave and Mrs Tapper leases the shop to Doreen Glinn who buys the freehold in 1965 and continues running the shop until 1988 when she retires, accepting an offer from Plymouth City Council for the property. The Lake Stores remains the property of PCC who currently lease it to William McMonagle.

"Mum and dad were married on the 7th June 1937, and lived at 10 Alfred Street, the Hoe. Mum worked in the accounts department of Spooners and dad was working as a van salesman for Liptons the grocers. My parents decided to take on the shop, probably to earn some extra money as Mum was getting just five shillings a week [25p]. I think it was dad's idea initially so they leased it from Mrs Tapper and moved there in 1939. They ran it together to start with but soon after mum ran the shop on her own and dad went to work for Millbay Laundry as a despatch manager, the job he had when I was born.

During the war we had railway sleepers in the rear garden, stacked against the back wall, so we could get over into the farm and use their air raid shelter which was just the other side of our back wall. It was half above and half below ground level as I remember. We were sheltering in there one night and some bombs dropped very close by. The whole thing shook violently. I suppose I was too young to be really frightened. If we had enough warning we used to go over to Mr and Mrs Ralph who had a bungalow along Barton Road, Number 4, because they had an underground shelter with running water and electricity. It was built into the front garden. He had most of the front garden done in chippings with gladioli down the centre.

Mr and Mrs Thorn, who bought 4 Barton Road in 1963 from Mr Moore, who had bought it from Mr Ralph, said "It was still there when we bought the bungalow. Quite a big shelter, built against the ter-

ABOVE: The Lake Stores, 15th March 2001.

RIGHT: In 1948. L. to R. Barbara, Josephine, Brian and Stephen Mahon.
Ices, lollies and ice cream sodas are served from the tip up window on the left. Ice creams are 3d and 6d and cream sodas are 6d. The metal swing sign under the right hand window is for Martin's Dairy Ice Cream of Looe.

race wall of the front garden and dug down into the ground to give about 2 metres height inside. There were trees and bushes growing on top of it, steps down and around to a door. It was built of concrete block and showing signs of collapse; as we had a lot of young children around at the time we thought it safer to demolish it and fill it in."

Above: 1942. Barbara Mahon in the garden of 4 Barton Road. Below, the background enlarged.

Air Raid shelter (shrapnel protection)	Private Road Sign	A R P Water tank	Tapley's showground	Farmhouse and Barn

Dad wasn't eligible for call-up because he had a heart condition and poor eyesight caused by rheumatic fever but he did his bit as an officer in the Home Guard. When we were clearing out the shop to move in 1951 we found this big tin of ammunition. Mum had a fit!

I remember rationing of course, counting the coupons. I think a lot of barter went on during the war. I seem to remember a lot of Rabbit pie and Rabbit stew. I think the farm used to supply us with milk during the war and I can remember my mother making cream, not to sell but for our own use.

When the shop was open on a Sunday Mum used to put us on the bus. Up on the top deck at the front and we'd ride to Saltash Passage and back. A shilling [5p] I think it was.

We were cut off for six weeks in the bad winter of 1947 because very little could get up Radford Dip, certainly not the buses, because of the snow.

Childhood was great there. I was mostly in the farm, with the Ralphs or up Church Hill with Dr. Schmidt, a German lady doctor. I used to spend a lot of time

out of the shop, being looked after by families in the village. Our cat Kitty populated the village with her kittens. If I wasn't playing in the farm I was trying to go to [Hooe Primary] school with the other children, 'course I was too young then! I used to play with the children in the village. All the churches seemed to work together then. We were in the minority as Catholics and we went up to St. Gregory's in Plymstock. I had an accident on the way to church in July 1950, the Sunday after the slow bike race at the back of Harris' Tea Gardens. Brian was with me. The buses only came every hour and we had missed one. We were determined not to miss Mass and so we cycled. Just up from Hooe Chapel a car clipped the back of my right hand. A Morris 8 series E it was with the backdoor handle pointed forward and it was that which caught me. It made quite a mess of my hand. Didn't knock me off my bike though. The driver was a policeman from the MoD base at Turnchapel going home to Oreston. Brian rode back to the shop to tell my father who came with me in the ambulance to hospital.

We used to swim in the lake. You'd wait for the tide to come right in so you could swim a width without getting muddy.

The farm was run by Mr and Mrs Ford and Mrs Ford's mother. Then there was Harry Burgoyne their helper and I have a feeling that Herbert Rendle worked there at one time. They had a huge great white horse that they used on the farm. If my memory serves me right I think Mr Ford used to ride the horse as well. The very young animals were kept in the Barn and it was also used for storage, fodder for the animals and such. There seemed to be keen competition between them and Rogers at Barn Farm.

They used to own and race greyhounds, Jack Ford and his wife. I got bitten by one. She had pups, I should have known better! Jessie she was called. They had a vegetable garden at the rear of the farm where they also had a run for their turkeys. Mrs Ford had some nasty turkeys there, nasty in terms of bad tempered you know. At the back of the farm they had a lean-to place where they killed and plucked them and chickens, I can remember plucking chickens myself. Then you'd go through another arch from that garden out through an orchard to the fields.

They had flagstone floors in the farmhouse. I used to play up on the Brakes, mind you it was just brambles and scrub. I can remember Mrs Ford making butter and using the butter pats.

When you entered The Lake Stores the shop itself was on the left. Behind the counter was a passageway. To the left of the passageway was the kitchen which had a bath with a removable cover and a gas geyser. To the right of the passageway at the back was Brian's and my bedroom. At the front on the right was the lounge with a Put-U-Up for mum and dad. Very basic. Coal fires, septic tank and outside toilet. At some stage Dad grew vegetables or something out the back but they didn't do much with that as dad was working all the time now.

When the water was cut off for some reason, perhaps in the winter when the pipes used to freeze, we used to collect water from the spring beside the shop [Shute Quay], that kept us going a few times. I was gassed once as a baby. My mother, getting up on hearing me cry, saved us all because the gas main had broken under the shop.

We had a big gas refrigerator in the shop and a water rat got into the works. We had to call Mr Stevens the butcher and he came over. He must have decapitated the thing.

We used to sell Martin's Dairy Ice Creams from Looe and mum used to make her own ice lollies and ice cream sodas. Had tables outside, round metal green ones with wood and metal folding seats. We made teas for the bus drivers and conductors, because Hooe was the terminus then. The buses went a bus length up Church Hill, reversed down into Barton Road and then stopped opposite the shop for about 10 minutes. We had one cat that was absolutely enormous called Panda, one of Kitty's kittens. He was huge, just like a big Cheshire cat. This bus driver wanted him and in the end mother gave it to him. A couple of weeks later he said "I know why you let me have that cat, he's eating me out of house and home."

Break-ins, burglaries were rarely heard of in the area and we had no trouble in the shop, well we lived on the premises. I went to Hooe School for about a year when I was four. They let me in early because I was such a pest trying to get in. Then I went to Holy Cross in Plymouth. Margaret Barter, her parents had the Hooe Social club, she was a bit older than me and she used to walk with me to the train and to school until I was old enough to go by myself. In the summer I'd sometimes get the Ferry from Turnchapel to Phoenix Wharf and walk from there to school.

I stayed at Holy Cross until I was eleven, did my eleven plus and went to Notre Dame, but by that time we had left Hooe and were living in Plymouth.

We went to a wholesaler in Notte Street for cigarettes and tobacco, I used to be lifted up and sat on the counter while they were ordering the cigarettes but the rest used to get delivered. Fruit and Veg. came from Drakes wholesalers in Plymouth. We sold cold meats, mainly corned beef and ham that came in big tins and had to be sliced up. Dried fruit and sugar came in bulk and had to weighed out into bags on a pair of scales with a platform for the weights on one side and a scoop on the other. There was a separate larger set for potatoes and vegetables. Masons Lemonade was delivered by lorry with the bottles in wooden crates. The bottles had a 2d [just under 1 new penny] deposit on them. There was a cheese cutter with a wire and wooden handle. We sold slices of Lyons cakes and Scribona sponges that were cut from a large slab of cake. Sweets like sherbet and sherbet lollies and Drake's Cushions were sold loose from jars or boxes and there were tins of Blue Bird and Devon Cream toffees. There was also toffee in trays that had to be broken up with a small toffee hammer. Paper bags were very hard to get hold of. I remember sheets of greaseproof being cut into squares and mother making cones from this for the sweet bags. Vegetables and dried fruit were seasonal. Sugar and Rice were sold loose and weighed into bags. Mushrooms, blackberries and watercress were picked from the fields. We also sold pickling vinegar loose and customers would bring their own bottles to be filled. Mum seemed to be open all hours. Especially after the war.

Sharps Toffee Hammer

Mum and dad had a silver tray presented to them by a couple of the Canadian airmen who were stationed at Mount Batten and billeted at 4 Westway 'To Jo and Steve with best wishes. From the Canadians. 4 Westways. 1942.' and the crest of the Royal Canadian Air Force. My brother's got it now. I can remember soldiers being stationed at Fort Stamford. It was a very close knit community because it was so small.

I remember Mr and Mrs Morrow in 1 Westway, Mrs Birch, Mrs Schmidt the doctor. I believe she left the country during the war. Mum kept in touch with her for a while but they lost touch after the war. Professor Waterfield at number 2 Barton Road, he taught music and played the organ at St. Andrew's in Plymouth. A tiny man he was, with a goatee beard. Savery had a fish and chip shop and there was a Social Club where Harris Court houses are now. That and St. John's Church hall were the centres of social activity. They used have old time dancing there and the RAF personnel used to come up from Mount Batten and join in. There were also concerts held at St. John's Hall, there was a stage at one end. Mum and dad were keen singers and used to do all the Nelson Eddy and Jeanette Macdonald songs. I met my husband, Tom, while in the audience listening to mum and dad sing.

My brother Brian was born in the shop. I was sent over to Mrs Ralph's until it was all over. When he was about six months old he had an abscess. We thought that it was the lancing of this and some subsequent infection that led to him catching Polio. He was in hospital a long time with this, about two years I think. When he came back he didn't know us. He had his leg in a calliper for a long time and had to wear a special boot at night to immobilise his foot, because that's how they used to treat it then. Ingrid Larcombe said to my mum, "Throw all those things away. Get some water from the Lake, boil it up and make him swim in it." Exercise it in sea water. Mum did that and he got a lot better. If he hadn't his leg and foot would have been a lot worse. He had a dropped foot but that was stabilised when he was twelve.

The reason we left Hooe was because the living accommodation in The Lake Stores was too small. I was going on 12 and needed a room of my own. In 1948 my father was taken ill with inflammation of the lining of the heart caused by a leaking heart valve, the result of rheumatic fever he had when he was seventeen. The illness meant that he was in hospital for a long time and off work for six months. In the space of two weeks I had the road accident, my grandmother had died. I think this was the start of mum wanting to leave the shop.

My mother's sisters each had a flat in a three storey house in Plymouth and one of these came available so we moved into that one. Dad carried on as the transport manager for Millbay Laundry and mum went back to work in the accounts department in Spooners. 1951 that was. Doreen Glinn, who used to help out in the shop took up the lease and later bought the shop."

DOREEN GLINN

"I started work by working for Edna Sherrell, the florists. The first shop she had was in Drake Street. That was a street that led into the market that got blitzed. Then she went up to Saltash Street.

Edna and I were very great friends, we used to go on holiday together. I was always keen on getting a shop. This one my cousin owned and when it came that the people in it left I took the shop. It was a general store run by Mrs Mahon. She had a son and daughter. I think the son, Brian, runs a newsagents on Mutley Plain, and they all lived in there. I helped out in there for a while.

I took it over in 1951 and ran it until 1988 when Plymouth City Council made me an offer I couldn't refuse, so I sort of retired.

It was already called The Lake Stores when I took it over but the actual name of the building was Harwin. It was called that after my cousin. She was called Winifred and her husband was called Harry. When I used to get the rates demands from Plymouth City it would be addressed sometimes to The Lake Stores, sometimes to Harwin.

I never closed when there was that accident and the oil tank caught fire in 1970. Lots of people were evacuated because of the danger of an explosion but I didn't go.

If you ever look in the attic of that shop you'll find it filled with barbed wire. I was always getting burgled, mostly they'd break in through the door or a

L. to R.
Josephine, Barbara, Brian and Stephen Mahon in 1948. Hooe Lake, swing bridge and tethered oil drums in the background

Rear of The Lake Stores, 23rd February 2001. The new tiles covering the burglary entrance are still clearly visible. The small lean-to room is the outside toilet.

window but once they took a piece of the roof off, got in and stole cigarettes, tobacco and a big slab of cheese. Anything they could get really. You can still see the patch of replacement tiles. The insurance people kicked me out, wouldn't insure me anymore because of the number of burglaries. They caught someone after two years and they had to go to court in Plympton. I remember going to court and seeing this scruffy pair walking along the street. I said to my friend who was with me at the time "I bet it's those two." and she said "No, no, not them." But when we got into court there they were, it *was* them. They were as scruffy as anything! They caught them in Bristol. I was worried stiff having to stand up in the witness box and of course I wasn't speaking very loud. The Magistrate said "Speak up so we can all hear" but I was frightened for my life.

Then there was a dentist living down the road gave me dud cheques. There was a building society man lived up Higher Hooe, he did dud cheques too. Mrs. Flanders had some. I went down the Police Station ten o'clock one night to identify this bloke. He was going to leave the country. Other than that it was just hard work and happy days. I used to open at nine in the morning until seven or eight in the evening. In the summer I used to open later. Everyday of the week.

When the troops all came for the Suez War embarkation I had loads and loads of soldiers here. They all came into the shop for cups of tea. Of course I had lots of cups and saucers but not enough for that lot! There was a man called Bill Pearce that lived up near the chapel, he was knocking on my door about five o'clock one morning saying "Come down and open up because there's soldiers down there for cups of tea." So I opened up and he went out the back washing up the cups.

The Garage did a few newspapers when I first came here, there wasn't another shop. I was given to understand that when I bought my shop that was the last one on the boundaries of the shopping area.

When I was in hospital recently this lady kept looking at me. She said "I know your face but I can't place you. Where do you live?" I said "Hooe" she said "That little shop down by the bus stop!" She recognised me and her children are forty years old now. They used to come into the shop, there was four families, they came from Camel's Head, they all used to come in buying penny lollipops. All go up the beach all the families together then when they used to come home in the evenings they all used come across while they were waiting for the bus and have another penny lollipop. I said "One of your boys got terribly burned in the face." "Oh," she said "he grew up to be a lovely man, all cleared up." That was terribly sad, another kid threw a match into some fireworks and they all went up. She recognised me from forty years ago so I couldn't have altered much!

I always had someone in my shop. It seemed to be never empty. I could never sit down for half an hour, there was always someone there. Happy days though. I never regretted it.

1956. Sept / Oct. The Suez Crisis. Tanks and troops in the entrance to Hooe Lake Quarry, Barton Road, waiting for embarkation at Sycamore Beach, Turnchapel. The then disused chute for loading barges with stone and lime can be seen in the background

When they were filling in the end of the lake Mrs Elford came down very upset about it. "Still," she said, "it is progress." So I didn't say any more. Then a little while after what happened? They [the Elfords] went and built all those bungalows opposite me so she came in one day about the bungalows and I said "Well it is progress isn't it?" Of course I meant it as a hint about filling in the lake. That infilling spoiled the character of the village. The water's lovely and now everyone's clamouring to get near it.

I got milk for the shop from Unigate. When the supermarket opened on the Broadway they were selling milk for less than I could buy it wholesale from Unigate. I phoned up but couldn't get no sense from them and someone gave me the direct line to the head office at Totnes. The man there said "Well of course the supermarket takes a lot more!" Well I was taking around 100 pints of a Sunday and I asked if they valued their old customers. Oh didn't he go wild. He was livid and asked who had given me his direct line. I was going to finish with them because I could just as well get it from the supermarket and sell it on.

I used to get some fresh milk from the farm, for my own use, Mrs Ford would put a can of milk on the garden wall.

Harry Burridge used to go around with a hand cart full of swedes or turnips. We used to get 5 or 6 turnips for sixpence [2.5 new pence]. When you think of it how many would go around now with a cart selling turnips? I suppose it was the pleasure of doing it and a few pennies. They used to grow them up on top of the warren, that's where Tapson Drive is now, on top of the Quarry. They used to till that.

Just at the end of the Barn there was a wall running across and they used to stack mangols for the cattle and cover them over with old bushes to protect them. When it came to Guy Fawkes day the kids used to reach in and try to take one for a lantern. Of course if you'd gone and asked for one they'd have given it to you but it was more fun to take one I suppose.

We were told not to walk on [the east side] of the Brakes because it was dangerous, something to do with the reservoirs there I think."

POROSAN

PRESERVES

Make delicious reserves

Fruit is always a welcome addition to the diet. But especially so when it is scarce. Palm pressure on POROSAN Rings and Caps will enable you to preserve surplus fruit in ordinary 1 and 2 lb. jam jars successfully without any fuss or trouble. For jars of irregular shapes and sizes use POROSAN No. 1 Skin for a perfectly airtight seal. POROSAN Methods never fail if the simple directions are followed.

Marketed by:

POROSAN LIMITED. 65/66. Chancery Lane, W.C.2.

POROSAN
Fruit Preserving
METHODS ARE BEST

Cookiemalt

BRINGS OUT THE BEST IN SAVOURIES SWEETS & DRINKS

MALT EXTRACT SPECIALLY MADE FOR THE KITCHEN

NO POINTS 1/9 *per lb. jar*

Hooe Barton Garage & Shop

1934. Hercules Doddridge buys the strip of land around the North and East sides of the Barn from Ernest Sherrell, owner of Hooe Barton farm. He is buying it for his son, Hedley, who is training to be an engineer. The lean-to garage building is completed in 1935. The small concrete extension to the west being used to recharge radio accumulators and other batteries.

Hedley Doddridge serves in the second world war but returns 'a changed man' and his heart is not in running a garage.

1946 (circa). Hedley Doddridge sells the land and premises to Frank Rogers, who lives in Manor farm, Staddiscombe. Frank Rogers divides the west part of the garage off for a Newsagents Shop and circa 1947 leases the Garage to Chris Willdern, keeping Barton Shop and the associated paper round separate, to be run by himself.

Chris Willdern's father, who had retired from the Western National Bus Company, works in the Garage occasionally and is known as Pop.

1962-1965. Mr Gordon and Mrs Doris Vanstone take up the lease for Barton Shop from Frank Rogers who concentrates on Barn farm. Doris says: "We saw it advertised and thought we could make a go of it. We were just moving to Plympton at the time. I had worked in shops before so knew the business. It was OK but very small, you couldn't carry the stock. Then the shops on the Broadway opened up and that sort of killed it off. At the time it was just newspapers, cigarettes and sweets. We gave it up and I went to work for Willcock's in Plympton and my husband, Gordon, had a vegetable round. Mr and Mrs Hancock took over Barton Shop after us."

1970. The Willderns retire and the lease is taken up by David Butler, who runs it for a year then emigrates to Australia in 1971.

1971 William Ernest McMonagle takes up the lease and runs the garage and paper shop to the present day (2001)

1994. June 14th Frank Rogers dies and the property passes to his daughter Jacqueline, now Mrs Jacqueline Truscott.

Jacqueline Truscott (nee Rogers)

"Dad was born down at Gabber. The family then moved to a bungalow at Staddiscombe, it was a green corrugated iron bungalow, where the large bungalow on the corner is now. It was about the size of a small pre-fab. When my father was one year old his father died, August the first 1914. His

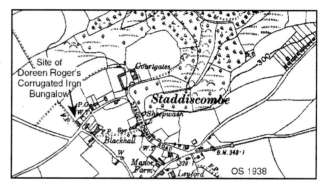

mother would have had a lot to contend with then and they were all very lucky not to have been put into a home. They were very, very poor. They didn't have shoes and dad had to go out farm labouring. Somehow or other he got some money together to buy the land for a shop and what would be Staddiscombe Post Office and Newsagents. It's still

Frank Rogers in 1983, aged 70. Photo Jacqueline Truscott.

there on the right as you come into Staddiscombe from Goosewell. He liked dealing with papers and counting, it had a fascination for him. He also wanted to build up a small-holding there, with chickens and pigs and things like that.

When he was called up for the war, he'd be about 26, he tried to get out of it by saying he had a farm to look after [that would count as a reserved occupation and so be exempt from call-up] but they said

Doreen Rogers cutting her 60th birthday cake. Photo Jacqueline Truscott.

it wasn't big enough, so he had to go. He proposed to mum (Annie Doreen), who was living in Plymouth at the time and working for Brendon's Printers, but she didn't want to marry him then because he was going away on call-up. When he went away his mother took over the shop and ran it throughout the war and my mum went there to help out a bit. Then he must have come back for some leave and they got married. My mum was always known as Doreen.

My mum moved out at Dousland with her mother. She used to go out cleaning in all the big houses to pay some of the mortgage on Staddiscombe Post Office so it would be there when dad came back from the war. Dad drove big Army transports during the war. When he came back he got locked up quite a bit because he wouldn't do as he was told. He wasn't that kind of man, more of his own man like. When my mum went up to Scotland to see him (because

he was going to be demobbed from there) he always seemed to be in the glasshouse. She would be told he'd been a bad boy again, he just wouldn't toe the line at all.

It seems to me they sold the paper shop at Staddiscombe to buy Manor farm around 1952 but they would have had to keep the newspapers going. What they probably did was keep the newspapers running from Manor farm, because I can remember stacks of newspapers in the Linhay and cutting the tops off the unsold ones because you only got rebated on the returns if they had the tops cut off. Then they bought the garage and shop in Hooe and moved all the papers down there. The Garage was called Hooe Barton Garage and the shop, such as it was, Hooe Barton Shop.

Mum used to have a bed and breakfast here at Manor farm. Dad used to get up at six o'clock to do the papers at Hooe, mum would get up to start the breakfasts, Dad would to do the vegetables, his son John would be doing all the farm work, milking the cows and everything. Mum would go down the Hooe shop after she'd done the bed and breakfasts and dad would come home and go down to pick her up about ten o'clock at night.

Mum didn't have enough money to properly stock the shop as she would have liked. This salesman from Macintosh Sweets came in and said "Let me stock your shop." She said "No, I can't afford it. My husband would go mad!" and he said "Let me stock it because a sweet shop will not run unless it's well stocked. Don't worry about the money!" So she took the plunge and had it stocked up. Then she sort of lived on a knife edge for a while, worrying about the money, but it did take off and she did really well and had a thriving business. Then they went into a bit of fruit and veg that dad was growing at Manor farm. I can remember big scales outside for weighing the potatoes. The vegetables were all stacked up to the bottom of the window.

Hooe Barton Garage and Shop in 1999. At this time the Garage and Shop are leased by William Ernest McMonagle from Jacqueline Truscott.

I used to go down the shop regularly, used to almost live in a cardboard box. I seem to remember lots of Dolly Mixtures and Barker and Dobson sweets. I was there day and night from the age of four, well it was a way of life, my mum had to look after me of course so I came with her. As the years went on they managed to buy Barn farm and in 1956 he let Barton Shop too. The rents from both helped keep the farms going.

When we had Barn farm then pigs came into it and dad was a pig man in a big way. He used to get all the contracts for left-over food from Goodbodys, RAF Mount Batten, RAF Collaton Cross and the Gas Board, in fact anywhere where we could get a couple of bins of swill and we used to drive around and collect those. Bread from Goodbodys could only be collected on Mondays, Wednesdays and Fridays and we couldn't go in until seven in the evening. We used to take our old van with ten big hessian sacks, driving into the bakery when everyone was coming out. There would be huge baskets filled with bread and cakes that they'd just tipped in. Dad would hold the sack and I used to fill it up, I got into such a swing that we got the job done in about an hour and a half. I did that from the age of eight to nine years old right up until I was fifteen.

We'd be lucky to get home much before 10 o'clock at night. The car would break down often, well we just didn't have the money to keep the things maintained. My brother would get the tractor out and tow it back. Even though we owned the land the Garage stood on, McMonagle was working there then and of course people still needed to be paid for their work.

Then we went back to run Barton Shop again. The lease must have expired and dad went back to run it because he had to get the paper business back. I remember something about that because Mr and Mrs Hancock, who lived in 6 Barton Road, were running newspapers from their bungalow. They had run the shop from 1960-66. Dad always had this horror of the newspaper business leaving the shop.

John and Bill, Frank's brothers, helped a bit with the paper rounds. Bill did a round with his bike around Langdon Court. On the way back he stopped to have a drink, count the money or something. Anyway, when he got back to the shop he realised he didn't have the money and must have left it where he'd stopped, so he got back on his bike and rode all the way back, about three miles, and there it was in the middle of the road. The bikes were like butchers bikes with a basket on the front.

We went to Barn farm 1959/60. I was in Notre Dame school at the time and came home to find all the furniture packed up at Manor farm, which was a bit of a surprise as I didn't know we were moving.

Mum wasn't a very good driver. We had this old cash till in the back room, really old fashioned one it was and we could never open it. One day she was driving the car and realised she hadn't got her handbag. Turned round to look in the back seat to see if it was there and hit the wall an almighty wallop and the old cash till, which was on the other side, opened.

The shop has always been the same inside, same size and everything. Water tended to come in on spring tides, and it also filled up the inspection pit in the Garage.
I remember once Dad said to me "Run after that boy! He's pinched some sweets!" and I chased him up to the Hooe toilets. What I was going to do with him if I caught him I don't know but I ran after him 'cause dad said 'run'.

The shop was broken into once around 1958 and they took almost everything. The Police said they couldn't help but dad wouldn't let it go. He toured all the sweet shops in the area looking for his stock, you see the sweet boxes were marked with our shop's name. Well he found them in a shop in Torpoint and got the police to go and get them."

BRIAN WILLDERN

Chris and Brian Willdern ran Barton Garage from 1947-1970. Chris died in 1994

"Chris was the one who took up Barton Garage, renting it from Frank Rogers soon after he (Frank) bought it from Hedley Doddridge. About 1947 that was and Chris would have been 30, I joined him working at the Garage about 13 years later in 1960, and our father, 'Pop', who was retired from the Western National, used to help out too.

We used the name Barton Garage, it might have been called that already. It was a really smelly place when my brother first moved in; it was a real hovel, being built on the side of the barn. If Jack Ford swabbed out in the Barn all the wash used to come through, the drains came through the walls into the Garage you see, so we had that smell to put up with quite often. It was an earth floor and it was damp all the time, and cold. If you did put down some concrete it used to break up for some reason. We were always working on the floor. If you had to get under a car it was put up on stands and you were on the floor all the time. There was no pit or a lift though we did have a girder across with a block and tackle on it for lifting out engines. It ran from above the window behind the pumps into the big buttress of the Barn.

We had a big paraffin tank in the corner, up on a stand. I used to go around doing paraffin deliveries for people with heaters. The garage had a single skin galvanised roof, well it still has, and it was so cold in the winter and it used to sweat. At that time the shop was all part of the Garage and where the small concrete extension is, to the right as you stand in front of the shop, that's where we used to charge

Fordson Major Tractor

accumulators. Everyone was on accumulators then for radios and we used to have banks of them on charge. Then when the shop was partitioned off we moved all that down the east side of the garage. We didn't use the east shippon because that was Jack Ford's. Jack was into greyhounds; almost every Wednesday he was rushing to get away to Exeter or some track. I've been caught a couple of times, Jack or Winnie would come into the Garage and say "Brian, come in the shippon, a cow's calving" and I'd go into the east shippon and help pull the calf

South end of Hooe Lake 1938. Mr and Mrs Mahon have just taken over Lake Stores and Hercules Doddridge is running the Garage. The two tall petrol pumps are tucked under the canopy, which does not have a name board on it, and flank an oil bin.
Shute Quay is a well defined structure. The balk of timber in the forground is adrift from Bayly's seasoning pontoon.
Railings around the lake wall will be put up in 1940. Photo courtesy of Barbara Jennings.

out and think 'this is good isn't it? I'm supposed to be repairing cars.' We had quite a lot of dealings with the Jack over one thing and another.

That shippon in the Farm, the one next to Tapley's, I can remember that being full of tins of grease, dozens and dozens of them, about 14lb (6.35 kilo) tins they were.

Jack had a lovely old tractor, a Fordson major, used to chug along. Roy Hopper used to collect lots of farm equipment and in the end he was using his machinery for Jack.

There were two petrol pumps there for years, tall ones. We put in a third new low one in the middle. The majority of our work and petrol sales came from the servicemen at RAF Mount Batten. You get all sorts as customers and of course being a small business you have to be nice to everyone.

We got our fresh water from the outflow at Shute Quay. We had no running water in the garage and we were very lucky that the water at Shute Quay was there because it ran all year round regardless of weather. It was so pure you could use it for distilled water in the batteries and accumulators. That was tested by the people at Mount Batten and was found to be that pure. Good stuff. We used to park cars in that space and we used the public toilets just down the road because there were none in the Garage.

Chris learned his trade by working for W. Mumford's [garages] after leaving school. He always wanted to be an engineer and that's what he started off at with Mumford's in their workshops out at Salisbury Road [runs from Beaumont Park to Mount Gould Hospital]. Back in those days you were a tied apprentice and Mumford's said they had promised the mechanic's apprenticeship to someone else and would he mind changing his trade to a coachbuilder, which he did and spent many years coachbuilding. Then during the war he was working for Mumford's at their Billacombe works building aircraft. Spent most of his time making up the jigs for the aircraft. After the war he went back to coachbuilding again, though for a period he was working in the Abbey Garage because Mumford's had a contract for overhauling the engines that came out of sunk or damaged landing craft. He spent many years there doing that. Then he started to suffer from his nerves, packed it in at Mumford's and started a small garage business about half way along Dean Park Road, Plymstock, doing car repairs and servicing.

If you turn up Dean Park Road, coming from Hooe, the road slopes up then levels off for a short while before rising again. Just at that point there was a plot of land on the left where Mr Howard, the owner

of the land, had built this garage out of the corrugated iron from old Anderson air raid shelters. It was quite a big place, with double doors so Chris took that on doing car repairs. But being in a residential area there were complaints to the council about noise and one thing and another. People just didn't like the idea of a garage business being built up among the houses.

Frank Rogers was one of his customers, he had the paper round that covered that area. He asked him one day if he would like to run his garage at Hooe; the Hooe garage had petrol sales and there were always complaints about the noise and one thing and another regarding the garage in Dean Park Road so he took up the offer. Trouble was they did it by gentleman's agreement, there was no proper legal lease. That was OK for twenty years or so, then...

Frank Roger's son John was getting married and that's about when Frank wanted to get us out of the Hooe garage. Frank used to sit himself around the lake and watch people coming in for petrol. He always used to say it was a gold mine. He wanted to get my brother out so he could run the garage himself because he was of the opinion that the garage would better help subsidise the farm if he was running it himself; apparently he couldn't make enough out of Barn Farm alone to support John. Of course he knew little about doing garage work himself, maybe he planned to employ a mechanic.

Anyway what happened was it went to court and we could see that Frank would win the case, us not having a proper legally drawn up lease, so we got out. [1970] Frank didn't run it himself, he leased the Garage to Dave Butler who ran it for about eighteen months as Butler Engineering before selling the lease and his house in Pollards Close to 'Mac' McMonagle and emigrating to Australia [in 1971].

When we got out of the garage we went over to what was Hooe Bakery, in the village, what was Harwood's then it was Taylor then there was another baker, Medlin, who finished up and sold it. That's when they did away with Doddridge's house. As you went around the corner by the Royal Oak there was a square with all the cottages around and facing you was a big house, that was Doddridge's, the chap who built the Garage for his son. All new houses now.

Chris did car repairs there for a couple of years then packed it up again because there were objections from the council about noise and it being a residential area, fire risk and so on, so he closed up and took on the off-licence in Dean Park Road. He had quite a big garage with those premises and he used to do the occasional bit of work there until he retired."

WILLIAM ERNEST 'MAC' MCMONAGLE

Originally from Southern Ireland 'Mac' has run the garage as 'McMullin Motors' since 1971.

"I was born in County Donegal, Ireland in April 1940. At 17, I left the family farm and travelled to Plymouth to serve my apprenticeship in Plymouth Dockyard where I joined the drawing office. In 1964, I left the dockyard and started up my own garage at Pennycomequick.

In 1968 I married Di, a Plymouth girl. She is a teacher and we had met at a dance while I was working in the Dockyard. Her family were keen swimmers and she went with them to Bovisand as a girl. She can remember waiting for the bus at Hooe, looking at the garage as it was then, not realising she would marry the man who would own it.

McMullin's Motors Garage in 1983. The car is a vintage Wolseley. Photo courtesy of Di McMonagle.

Around 1970/71 there was talk of a new flyover to be built where the garage at Pennycomequick stood. We discovered the business in Hooe for sale, liked the area and decided to buy it and move. However we still have the old garage as no flyover was ever built, although the area is now under development. The previous owner of the garage in Hooe, Dave Butler, planned to emigrate and offered to sell us his house in Pollard Close. Being conveniently situated behind the Garage, we accepted and became residents of Hooe. Two days after we moved in, we became the proud parents of our first daughter.

Before coming to Hooe, one of my suppliers kept saying that he couldn't spell 'McMonagle' and was going to use McMullin in future. The name stuck

and was registered. I've traded as McMullin Motors ever since.

I've employed many people over the years, many locals and some travelling from as far as Torquay and Dartmouth. Having the shop has given us the opportunity to employ young students. Watching their progress as they have followed on to careers has been interesting. We have written many a reference.

We continued to serve petrol for longer than most, as self-service became more common. The two original tall pumps were turned by hand, which was useful during electricity cuts. Eventually we had to update to newer models, which we still use today. The tanks are the original ones, three with 500 gallon capacity each. At first, we sold Shell and then Gulf Petrol, now its marine diesel as unfortunately it is no longer viable to sell petrol. One tank is filled with oil that is collected for disposal.

When we took over there was a very small pit here. It wasn't quite deep enough, so it had been built up around the sides to get sufficient height to stand under a vehicle. This meant that to drive a car over the pit you had to drive it up a ramp onto the low walls then down the ramp on the other side. As it was so small and kept flooding on spring tides, they abandoned it and filled in some of it with concrete. We made it deeper and bigger, though it was very hard going digging out two to three feet of concrete. We've made it deeper and lined it with concrete and it now has room for a workbench. It still gets water in slightly on exceptionally high tides, about twice a year.

Elsewhere in the garage we have changed the partition walls around slightly to make a bigger office out of two smaller ones. We have always repaired and serviced vehicles, including mechanical, electrical and bodywork. In our time here we have been on RAC, AA, and police emergency call-outs. We extended to hiring caravanettes, cars and, more recently, boat and caravan storage. We have been in the motor caravan hire for many years now; they continue to be an important part of our business.

In the past they have been hired for all sorts of reasons. Dr. Who or Tom Baker as he really is, used one of ours when he was filming Hound of the Baskerville's on Dartmoor. It was rather muddy there, he needed a shower and the caravanettes have showers in them. Liz Fraser looked in at the garage one day and Barbara Windsor showed an interest when she was shown around one on display in Plymouth. Caravanettes get loaned to charities, used by Ten Tors group leaders, transformed into exhibition vehicles by the council, accompany school groups, provide extra accommodation in people's drives, and even used for honeymoons.

Barton Shop was already separate when we first came and Molly Johnston leased it from Frank Rogers. Then she retired and we took it over. Originally it sold groceries, toys, papers and sweets, cigarettes and stationery.

It's not all been easy; in the early 50's, a nearly new van was stolen and we, a friend Ray Larson and I, ended up in Spain searching, finding and retrieving it. This was reported in the national as well as the local press.

We have seen many changes in our time, it's never been boring here; there have always been lots of interesting characters to meet, problems galore and now we wonder what will happen next."

Sheila Harris serving in Hooe Barton Shop. April 2001. She has worked in the shop for 7yrs. There are four paper boys and girls for the weekday morning and evening rounds and five on Sundays.

Garage forecourt 1992. Photo courtesy of Di McMonagle.

George Tapley

Frances Tapley talking about her father George Tapley who ran a monumental mason business from a workshop in a lean-to against the Barn. George was born in 1881 and died in Sept 1972.

"First of all my father had his workshop and display across the front of the barn, before the garage was built. About 1923 that would be. Mr Sherrell let him have some space there. Then Mr. Dodderidge bought the land to build a garage so Mr Sherrell let him have a

workshop at the side of the Barn, you know where the shops are now? Well the ones at the road end, opposite them the barn goes back, there are trees there now, well that's where he was. Mr Sherrell also let him have some land in the front, a little plot for a show ground.

He was always a mason but he said the monumental side was a bit slow at first and he had to take other jobs but then it came in hand over fist. He went to Wales to work on the reservoirs. He also worked on Castle Drogo, which isn't very old. When he was there he asked, for the men, if they could have a ha'penny an hour more pay [0.2 of a new penny] and he was given the sack! I mean, a ha'penny even in those days wasn't very much! In the war he worked at Mount Batten. He was like foreman of the works down there, he was in his sixties then. A bomb went through the breakwater and he had to get in a diving suit and go down to assess the damage. He went up in a Sunderland too, his friend took him up.

There's loads of things he did up in the churchyard. When the centenary of the Church was on he cut a plaque but the Reverend Pike wouldn't have it up the front, it's down the east end where nobody can see it.

He had a bit of a mild stroke and got over it alright and he made a keystone over the church to say when it was built. Sylvia Cooke's father went up with him to help fix it but he would go up the ladder himself.

And you see those houses opposite in Westway with the arches. He did all those arches. I think his father worked as a mason too.

There's dad with the head he carved in 1950. It was in the garden for thirty years and it was behind a tree and somebody pinched it. I could have howled because it was the only one, the only one he made. It was taken from the end of a Meerschaum pipe that my brother brought home from abroad, it's in his top pocket in the picture.

Dad, he used to carve all sorts of things. He did a monkey and it was out in the showground and when the Australians were here they pinched it and they were so drunk that father said they were found up in the middle of the road worshipping it. They were the Sunderland flying boat crews from Mount Batten. They were as wild as anything they were. They had a little car called Leaping Lena, it was only a little like square box thing, and they used to be crammed inside, riding on the running boards. They used to be up the pub waiting for it to open because the beer soon sold out and they'd be waiting for the next lot to come in. They were awful hard drinkers!

Next to the Chinese takeaway, that was the farm gate there. You went in that way, and on your right were the stables, then you went in further and the shippons were on your left and then you went up into where the house was and the dairy opposite. And there was an orchard up the back and there was a granary, which is, I suppose, about where the end of Pollard Close is, up in the field and it was on stone staddles to keep it up from the rats. I've been in there with my brother, it was a wooden floor and it was painted black. I can remember that one as plain as anything. I think I went just into the farmhouse, of course you were going there to buy milk and that so you'd go over to the dairy.

I'm on the left with Joy Robins. See there are no houses, just fields across there. This was taken in the front garden of No. 4 Church Hill in 1931 looking across the road. My father used to say he played football in there in hobnailed boots. There were big

elm trees all up Church Hill, lovely it was, really lovely. They were all taken down in 1936 when they built the houses. Of course the children thought it was alright, they could run along the trunks when they were on the ground. When they were building them Joy and I used to go over there to play. They had lots of putty for the windows and we used to put down a board and play shops and the like and baking with the putty and he happened to come up and he said "Oh and what are you doing then?" and we said "We're playing shops Mr Rowse." and he didn't say anything because we weren't vandalising it or anything like that. When they were building around the back, these bungalows along Amacre drive we was playing with a ball out there and I had wellington boots on and, of course, it went in the lime pit and I went in after it. One of the workmen there pulled me out and said "You'll get burnt!" and he hosed my boots down and all.

I remember they used to have hayricks in the fields there and of course they had horses for everything.

Edna and her husband used to live opposite in 10 Westway when they were first built which was 1937-38. Edna's husband died one Christmas. He wasn't very old, in his thirties, he had pneumonia. Edna sold the farm and went to Tenby to live. There's still an elm tree outside Sylvia Cook's house, which is called The Elms, but that particular tree is a younger one than the originals.

I remember an airship [R100?]. I was in the garden and I saw this great big yellow thing up in the sky. 1930 I suppose. I was very young. The other day I asked a friend, who is older than me, if I really had seen it and he said yes, because he remembered they had all had to come out of Prince Rock school to look at it.

We were all born in Hooe village. My brother was born in the little cottage next to the Post Office. He was down here one day and he noticed it was for sale and he said to the man in the garden "I was born in here." and the man said "Oh, were you? Would you like to come in and see?" and he went in to see. Course it was called Rose Cottage then, my Grandma had it.

I was only six weeks old when we came to this house. The cows kept breaking through the fence at the back and eating dad's cabbages. The house was brand new then, about 1927. Built by the Elfords. The bungalows along Barton Road were later, about 1931-5.

Talking about the quarrymen and horses picture on Page 59:
Bill [her brother] used to go over to the quarry and help on a Saturday. He wasn't very old. And that

was our entertainment. The boats used to come up for the stones from the quarry and they had a big chute on the quay over there and they used to shoot these stones down into the ship. We used to go and watch that, that was our entertainment, especially when the bridge opened to let a boat through. My mother said to me "Don't you go over there," she said, "those foreign ships, they'll take you away if you're not careful." We only went over there to watch the stones going down but Mother was really worried.

About the Paper shop. After Rogers had the shop Mr and Mrs Vanstone took it over, I think they lived round Plympton way. Then after that Mr and Mrs Johnson. She lives over Lalebrick Road now, then William McMonagle and he still runs it.

Harry Burridge used to work down at the farm as well. They used to come around with milk in the morning and milk in the afternoon. He used to come around with a churn and they used to dish it up with a can thing with a handle on it. Because people didn't have fridges in those days of course so they had to bring it fresh all the time. They did two milkings a day."

ERIC BURRIDGE

Eric worked for many years on the Turnchapel to Plymouth ferries but in his early days he helped out here and there for fun.

"I used to help out George Tapley making up stones in [Hooe Lake] Quarry. We'd get a lorry load of stones over from Radford Quarry, then put one in a tar barrel that was full of chippings, find a straight edge and mark up the four corners so as to be able to square it off and get the largest rectangular face from it. The edges would be dressed up but back behind it could be any shape. It was used for facing stones. That would be just after the war, George had a contract with A. N. Cole who were repairing the bomb damage around St. Jude's. Now all those houses are stone fronted so there's an awful lot of work to be done. They would say they wanted so many square yards of this and he'd make it up and they'd take it away. We never worked after 12 O'Clock, went to the pub after that. It was hard work but we never thought nothing of it."

Quarrymen with horses in Hooe Lake Quarry. Circa 1910. The man in the cap front left, without a horse, is Sammy Phillips "The Midget'. The man in the white shirt, braces and no waistcoat is George Dungey. Photo by Mr. Charlick, collection of Bill Tapley.

George and his brother worked the monumental masons' business by the Barn. He was a jobbing mason, well known, would make fonts and stones for churches, anything with stone, not just monumental work. He did the rocket house; you know, the coastguard depot by Tapson Drive.

All this business with the monkey started in 1941 when an incendiary bomb caught the corner of Hooe Manor [**Belle View**].

George Tapley's monkey 'Jack' in Eric Burridge's garden.

They caught them and we had to go to Plympton Court. The last public appearance of the cat, ferret and monkey was on the magistrate's bench.

After this George said to me they're not going to get pinched no more, here's yours [the monkey] and of the others one went to his brother and one to someone else."

The people who were there, the Grenvilles, did their best, poured water on it but they were hampered by the falling lead that was melting as well. The next day George had a call from Colonel Coates to go up and fix up the damaged stone. I think George was clerk of works at Mount Batten at the time and there were WAAFs billeted at Hooe Manor. Now Belle View/Hooe Manor was built from a fine French sandstone from Caen, same as Radford House was. It would be taken down the Caen canal and put onto ships at Ouistreham. It was used for many important buildings in Britain, Norwich Cathedral for one. It's very fine grain and doesn't discolour like Bath stone or Portland.

So he went up, fixed it and was clearing up when he thought that some pieces were too good to throw away and he could make something out of them. So he carved a Cat, a ferret and the monkey. I think he kept them in his garden, not in his showground by the Barn.

About the Australians taking them? I don't know, it was the war then and I was away at the time, but after the war, 1950-51 ish, three RAF chaps took the monkey, the cat and the ferret and I think George had had enough of all this and got the police in.

In 1922 George Tapley took this picture of a pair of his memorials in Hooe Churchyard. The bottom of the picture has been lost but the background shows the Baptist Church and Hooe road running up through fields.

CLAUDE DAMPIER
AND BILLIE CARLYLE

Claude Dampier, his partner Billie Carlyle and their terrier dog stayed in their caravan at the back of Sherrell's farm in August 1938. They were appearing at the Palace Theatre in Plymouth for a one week run from August 22nd - 26th. It was a very hot August and it seems likely that they extended their stay at the farm for a holiday because their visit is remembered as being for longer than a week.

PALACE, PLYMOUTH.
6.25. TONIGHT. 8.45.
Special Visit of the Famous
STAGE, RADIO, and SCREEN COMEDIAN.
CLAUDE DAMPIER
(Mrs. Gibson's Friend),
With BILLIE CARLYLE.
Supported by a Great Variety Show.
NO ADVANCE IN PRICES
Box Office 10 a.m. to 9 p.m.   Tel. 5347.

Claude Dampier was a popular stage, screen and radio comedian. He played the upper class twit, or professional idiot, something like Harry Enfield's 'Tim Nice-But-Dim', Cardew Robinson or Terry Thomas.

The review of his act at The Palace reads:
'Mr Claude Dampier, who, principally through the radio, has attained a popularity attained by few contemporary comedians, tops the bill at the Palace Theatre this week.
To see him on stage last evening [Monday August 22nd 1938] was to appreciate his happy sallies in full measure, and during the twenty-five minutes in which he and Miss Billie Carlyle were before the footlights the laughs were almost continuous. One of the funniest spectacles witnessed at The Palace for many weeks was that of the inimitable comedian and Miss Carlyle kneeling beside Mr Dampier's terrier, the three "singing" a well known carol.'

'Born Claude Connelly Cowan, in Clapham, London, 1879. He became a big star in Australia and South Africa (he spent seventeen years between the two countries) in the early years of the 20th century and didn't really crack it here until he met Billie Carlyle (born Doris Davy, Australia, 1902) in 1925. They teamed up as a double act, on and off stage, and came to the UK in 1927. They played Variety, and Claude became a popular character actor in films such as 'She Shall Have Music' in 1935 with Jack Hylton and June Clyde and 'Boys will be Boys' 1936 with Will Hay and Gordon Harker, 'Riding High' 1939, 'Don't Take it to Heart' 1944 and 'Meet Mr Malcolm in 1953. Channel Four sometimes shows them: if you spot one, do watch, for he was a very funny man and would have been as big a star today, with television a great medium for his wonderful face and real acting ability.

Claude had a friend he talked about whom we never saw. Rather like Dan Leno's 'Mrs Kelly' and, more recently, Hyacinth Bucket's son Sheridan, in "Keeping up Appearances". Claude's was 'Mrs Gibson'. It seemed a very funny name when spoken through his protruding teeth in that 'silly arse' voice. 'Mrs Gibson' happened through Claude forgetting part of a routine and simply saying the first name that came into his head. The audience liked it so it was kept in. His catch phrase became "I'll have to ask Mrs Gibson".

His material was occasionally 'Highly Sophisticated' i.e. filthy and he was banned from the Radio for three months for a remark about having to dash away because he had promised to squeeze Mrs Gibson's oranges.

Even though he was an excellent visual comic and Billie was a beautiful and perfect foil, it was radio that helped to establish Claude, Billie and 'Mrs Gibson' as national institutions.' (Hudd 1998)

It seems he was also a caravanning enthusiast, no doubt finding it useful to have a portable home when touring or on film location. His first was a special eighteen and a half foot long caravan built for him in 1937 by D.H. Morgan who made 'Fairway' caravans in Caernarfon. It boasted four pull-out sections, two each side of the caravan either side of the central wheels. When parked up these sections would be pulled out to give increased space inside. This gave the van a distinctive and memorable appearance. It was this van that Claude and Billie brought to Hooe Barton Farm. It was a heavy vehicle and needed a large car to tow it. Claude used a 4 litre Humber Super Snipe. In 1939 he had a larger Motorhome built on a Bedford M type 3-4 tonner chassis, with a slide-out section between the wheels. He gave both of his caravans the same nickname. SRM Nosbig. Yes, Mrs Gibson in reverse. He died in 1955 aged 76.

Billie Carlyle at Home

The Calor Gas Stove. It takes scarcely any space and is neatly recessed at the side of the writing desk.

A day-time settee fitted into one of the bays uncouples at night to make two single berths like this.

Mr. and Mrs. Claude Dampier (whose stage name is Billie Carlyle) have just taken delivery of this Fairway Special described on the page opposite.

(*Left*) The daily clean up takes only a fraction of the time that it does in a house.

Washing-up is not so bad when it can be done in front of a window letting in an enchanting view. Water is supplied through the tap by an electric motor.

(*Above*) Whilst on the road. Looking down the centre of the van when all the extending bays are not extended.
(*Below*) The Kitchen-End. The Vulcan gas cooker draws its gas supply from the Calor cylinder beneath. Under the sink is the 15-gallon water tank.

(*Above*) " For twelve years," says Mrs. Dampier, " my husband has been wanting a caravan like this. It's going to be so useful to us on our professional tours."

(*Right*) A peep through the front door. On the far side of the van is another door leading to the kitchen.

ABOVE: *Claude's Fairway van was so unique that it was the subject of this whole page review in 'The Caravan' magazine of September 1937. The slide out sections made the van more spacious but they necessitated a robust chassis and bodywork to support them, which made the van heavy for its size. Also they had watersealing problems and the idea was eventually dropped.*

RIGHT: *His replacement Carlight Special in 1947 with a central pull out section. L. to R: Claude Dampier, Billie Carlyle and an unknown woman.*

BELLE-VUE

Belle-Vue, the present 'Hooe Manor' at Higher Hooe.

This imposing Georgian house known for most of it's life as 'Belle-Vue', because it had one; see inside the front cover. The house has nothing to do with the original Hooe Manor at the head of Hooe Lake. It is thought that the name was changed to Hooe Manor by the Bulteels some time in the 1800's for reasons unknown but suspected as being to do with status and resale value.

The West Side that faces Hooe Lake.
(See inside Front Cover)

Over door detail.

There was a smallholding attached, the remains of which can be seen at the junction between Hooe Hill and Belle Vue Road.

Belle Vue was built in 1777 by Christopher Harris of Radford. It is built using French sandstone from the Caen area, the same stone that was used for Radford House. Harris died in 1786 but his daughter Anne continued to live in the house even after she married into the Bulteel family. Various Bulteels occupied the house until bankruptcy enforced their selling it to Colonel Coates around 1915.

It is now council flats and has been in council ownership of one sort or another since 1947. Immediately after conversion to flats in 1948 three of the five flats were secretly let to employees of Devon County Council. This caused some considerable disquiet and public protest, to no real effect of course although they did promise not to do it again.

63

NEWSPAPER REPORTS

WESTERN EVENING HERALD 7TH DECEMBER 1966

PRESERVE ANCIENT FARM, SAYS SOCIETY.

Plymstock's ancient Hooe Barton Farm - built in Tudor times and which may have been the site for a Saxon settlement - is threatened with extinction unless steps to preserve it by Plymstock and District Civic Society and the Old Plymouth Society succeed.

Messrs George Wimpey and Co., builders, have plans to build about six shops on the site. This would mean the demolition of the existing farm and buildings.

Plymstock Civic Society is asking that the local planning authority make a preservation order for the farm, its archway and barn. It would like to see the buildings put to some practical public use without destroying their historic connections. The society believes the farm and barn have possible uses with some conversion, as a youth centre, community centre or branch library.

Mr Stanley Goodman, a society member said Mr G. W. Copeland. a distinguished antiquarian and honorary archaeological consultant to the society, had expressed the opinion that the archway should be preserved in situ.

LAST TRACES

One idea was that the buildings should be incorporated into any constructions made at the site.

Mr. Goodman, who said the Devonshire Association was associating itself with the society's views, commented that at Hooe Barton there still remained the last traces of one of the most distinguished great houses in the Plymouth area.

He speculated what might be found underneath the turf near the farmhouse with careful archaeological research. It was just the sort of site the Saxons always used if they could.

The four-centred archway (1407 and possibly going back to 1100) was part of St. Anne's Chapel, from which the word Turnchapel was derived after earlier being known as Tan Chapel. This archway is depicted on the cap badge of children attending Hooe Junior School.

WESTERN EVENING HERALD 15TH DECEMBER 1966

PLANNERS ACT TO SAVE ANCIENT ARCH

The South-West Devon Divisional Planning Committee is to ask the Minister of Housing and Local Government to make a preservation order on the medieval archway at Hooe Barton Farm, Plymstock.

This was agreed at the committee's monthly meeting at which the outline plans of Messrs. George Wimpey and Co., builders, for six shops on the farm site were considered.

As previously reported, various people have sought to get the archway and tudor farmhouse and barn preserved because of their historical value.

The committee had before it representations from Plymstock Civic Society, the Old Plymouth Society, the Rev. L. E. H. Pike, former Vicar of Hooe and others.

Mr Pike recently wrote that the site had been occupied for about 900 years and was worthy of skilled excavation. It has also been suggested that the buildings could have some community use, perhaps as a youth club.

Mr J W. Turpin, planning officer, said today that the committee was still making inquiries into other aspects of the scheme, which would involve demolition of the farmhouse, barn and water trough.

If the Minister makes an order, the firm has the right of appeal, after which the Minister could order a local enquiry.

WESTERN EVENING HERALD 23RD JUNE 1967

CITY COUNCIL NEGLECT OF TUDOR FARM

Plymouth City Council is criticised for its lack of action over the future of Hooe Barton farm by Mr E. J. B. Lord, a trustee of the Hooe and Turnchapel Village Hall Society.

Because of a legal technicality, the preservation order on the Tudor farm and its buildings prepared by Plympton St. Mary Rural Council, was returned to the new authority for the area, Plymouth City Council.

64

"Yet, since the beginning of April until now," said Mr Lord "nothing has been done to present a fresh order. With vandals (as reported in Wednesday's Evening Herald) breaking up the building internally it is essential that authority be given for some sort of protection for the empty farm." says Mr Lord.

"The people we must blame for this are Plymouth for dragging their feet. It is perhaps the first occasion here when they have been able to demonstrate their superior efficiency. Let's see a bit of it."

For over 20 years the Village Hall Society has searched for a centre for the social and cultural activities of the district. To members Hooe Barton farm could be the ideal site.

A recent letter to the owners of the farm, Messrs. George Wimpey and Co from the Plymouth Planning Officer, Mr C.C.Gimingham, points out he is most anxious that no further damage occurs to the house, or the barn, and in particular that no vandalism takes place inside the house.

Mr Gimingham asks that ground-floor windows of the house be boarded up and that all reasonable steps be taken to prevent further deterioration of the property.

The Area Manager of Messrs Wimpey, Mr D.F.G. Loudoun, who want to demolish the farm and its buildings and erect six shops on the site, said it was very difficult to protect empty property against vandalism.

Mr Lord says, however, that the windows and doors could be bolted through with corrugated iron on the ground floor and the upper windows shut.
Mr Stanley Goodman, member of the Old Plymouth Society, offered the services of some young people to "police" the area at weekends, but Wimpey were not in favour of that said Mr Lord.

Western Evening Herald
12th December 1968

COMMUNITY CENTRE AT FARMHOUSE?

The question of whether the Hooe and Turnchapel area is to have a community centre at last was considered at a public meeting at Hooe Primary School last night, when local residents attended in force.

Mr T. E. J. Savery, who presided, said it was proposed to turn Hooe Barton Farm into a community centre and the present owners of the site, Messrs George Wimpey and Co. Ltd., had now agreed provisionally to lease it for 99 years to trustees to look after it at a rent of £5 a year.

It was a most generous offer, said Mr Savery, as there could otherwise be very good commercial use of the site by the company who had said they were not prepared to grant the lease to the old Hooe and Turnchapel Community Association as such.

"They are prepared, however, to grant a lease to a new body of local interests, which must be representative of the Hooe and Turnchapel Village Hall Association, the Plymouth Guild of Social Service, the Old Plymouth Society, the Plymstock Civic Society and at least two or three local councillors."

Mr Savery also said it was proposed to get the Village Hall Society going again but nothing had yet been settled. He paid tribute to Mr E.J.B. Lord, a trustee of the Village Hall Society.

During an hour's question time, Mr Lord pointed out that it had been agreed to appoint trustees to serve on the new association. The meeting was for the purpose of announcing the offer of the lease and to stress that in the meantime the property was deteriorating.

BURIAL GROUND
Mr Stanley Goodman, of the Old Plymouth Society, explained that the site included an archway which was early 15th century and which was undoubtedly part of the foundation of St. Anne's Chapel, which went back to 1415. The Tudor style farmhouse had been twice rebuilt, but the old barn was structurally quite sound. The main interest lay in the ground behind the farmhouse garden, which was almost certainly a Saxon burial ground. No one had ever dug it up but it was "a most exciting site."

Mr Goodman said he was prepared to bring people out in the Christmas holidays to start repair work, making the roof water-tight and clearing up the mess in the courtyard and he hoped local people would volunteer to help.

FUNDS
Announcing that a general meeting would be called later Mr Savery said it was hoped start work on the project by the early summer. The next step would be to get an architect and agree to plans with Messrs Wimpey and to see if the Village Hall Society and the Community Centre Association would be prepared to invest funds held by them in the new body. Government and local authority grants would also be available and he appealed for local support generally.

Small snags about the lease had still to be ironed out but in effect it was a gift to the area from Messrs Wimpey.

WESTERN EVENING HERALD
7TH FEBRUARY 1979

HOOE WANTS A BARN?
by Robert Earl

Devon Social Services Department has been asked by Plymouth City Council to see if it has a community use for the 600 year old Hooe Barton Barn.

A community centre was planned by a local association eight years ago, but it has never opened.

The move provides some encouragement to Hooe residents who have waited so long for action on converting the barn and more so for the Croydon owner of the adjoining shopping development whose supermarket premises, four shops, seven flats and a car park have remained empty and vandalised for the last five years.

The shopping centre is perhaps Plymouth's most expensively vandalised privately owned set of buildings and now resembles a combination of unauthorised local adventure playground with a vandals' paradise.

The grand concept in the early 1970's was that the barn would be converted to a community centre simultaneously with the occupation of the shopping centre.

Hooe and Turnchapel Community Association leased the barn at a peppercorn rent from the builders of a nearby estate.

The barn roof was renovated and other essential work done at a cost of about £1,600 by the association, but eight years later it is as vandalised as its newer neighbouring buildings.

SETBACK.
A director for the Croydon firm, who asked that his name should not be disclosed, said the shopping centre scheme had been set back by changed economic factors, including the emphasis now given by supermarket firms to larger shops, but he felt that if the community centre was in being, there would have been less vandalism.

He considered that if the local authority had been more helpful the vandal problems would have been minimised by tighter controls on access to the site.

He said damage at the shopping centre ran into thousands of pounds with broken windows, demolished walls, ripped off roof tiles and smashed lavatories.

"I have bricked entrances, covered in doorways, but nothing has stopped the vandals."

He added that if the community centre was in being the whole development would gel into something useful for Hooe, an area he felt was potentially one of the most attractive parts of Plymouth.

Mr Dennis Winfield, City Planning Officer, said the City Council could not be responsible for the security of the private property. This was the responsibility of the owner.

He added that the Planning Department had approached the Social Services Department to see if it might have a use for the barn following approaches from residents. The planners also had an interest in the barn because it was a listed building.

Mr Winfield said be did not consider the community use of the barn would the answer to the wider problems affecting the shopping centre. Mr Eric Lord, a trustee of the community association, confirmed that representatives of the Social Services Department had visited him to assess the potential of the barn project.

IMPRESSED.
Their move followed requests from local groups for facilities for a Young Wives group and other activities following the closure of the naval community centre with the rundown of the Admiralty married quarters at Hooe.

"They agreed there was a need for a community centre and were impressed with the barn scheme" said Mr Lord. The snags included the age old problem of finance, but there was a possibility of help from the civic lottery.

Mr Lord said it was also likely a public meeting would be called at Hooe to get residents involved once again in a project.

"I am now awaiting the results of the visit by the Social Services Department officers." he said.

The story of the community centre was one of disappointments and letdowns. He said the roof was almost as bad as it was before it was repaired, but it would be wasting money to repair it before the whole problem of the site was settled.

WESTERN EVENING HERALD
4TH DECEMBER 1986

HOOE BARN GUN CLUB PLAN ANGERS GARAGE MAN

The news that Hooe Barn, Plymstock is to have a community use as an air rifle club after years of neglect has angered adjoining garage owner William McMonagle.

He sees the development as another twist of the screw that will curtail his business McMullin Motors, and threaten the jobs of about 10 full and part-time workers as it will restrict vital parking and storage space. Mr McMonagle is angry because, he says, he has been thwarted in his own efforts to buy the barn and overcome the parking and storage problems which have cramped his business and caught him in a web of planning restraints.

The barn, a Grade 2 listed building, was leased many years ago at a peppercorn rent by George Wimpey, the builders, to a local group who saw a community potential there. The building was vandalised and never put to that use. Its deteriorating condition, together with the vandalised, run-down character of adjoining private shopping development that has remained empty for almost a decade, have led to many local complaints.

LOTTERY AID

Wimpeys have now agreed to repair the barn and sell it to Plymouth City Council for £150 to become the home of Hooe Barton and District Air Weapons Club.

The City Planning Committee also plans to spend about £4,000 from civic lottery funds on the barn. "I would have been willing to pay Wimpey far in excess of £150 and would have repaired the building and respected the preservation order", said Mr McMonagle.

Mr McMonagle and planning consultant, Mr Norman Mallett, feel the change of use of the barn is inconsistent with the refusals they have had for permission to park cars on two sites at the rear of the garage and beside the barn. "We have lodged an appeal with the Secretary of State for the Environment about the restrictions on parking." said Mr Mallett. He said the history of the Site showed that the garage had been there for about 50 years and that it was providing a much needed petrol and repairs service to a growing residential area. "To allow the business to survive as it is I need that parking space, even if I cannot use the barn for storage," said Mr. McMonagle. "The garage could not exist on petrol sales alone."

COMPLAINTS.

He agreed there had been complaints about unauthorised use of the barn for storage and about the parking of vehicles but felt these came from a very small number of residents. "Those people have even complained about petrol tankers turning in the public highway in Barton Road." said Mr. McMonagle. "I provide a 12-hour petrol and repairs service here every weekday in the only garage in Hooe."

Efforts to overcome the car parking problem by making use of available land, or by buying it, had been thwarted; even the existing frontage to the garage had been trimmed by County Council road improvements. Mr Mallett said: "In my opinion those roadworks should have realigned the other side of the road by the Green." He said the restrictions on McMullin Motors were not in the spirit of helping small businesses to survive and expand.

INCONSISTENT.

He also thought there was an inconsistency in allowing an air rifle club to use the barn when that would also generate its own traffic and noise.

Mr. Dennis Winfield, City Planning Officer, recalled that the Hooe Barton site had been the source of many complaints over a long period. He said there had been, contraventions by the garage of planning regulations through unauthorised parking and storage in the barn. Taken with the untidy, vandalised nature of the adjoining shopping development there had been problems which had required City Council action on several occasions in response to local complaints. "Wimpeys had leased the barn at a peppercorn rent for community purposes and it is difficult to see what objection there can be to the air weapons club." said Mr Winfield. "This is a genuine community purchase and the local community policeman is among those backing the project."

NO OBJECTIONS

Mr Winfield said he had received no planning application for the barn as a store by McMullin Motors and there had been no representations against the air weapons club application. He realised there was a parking problem for the garage but there had been an opportunity to have sorted things out when the shopping development was first mooted.

"The Planning Committee have felt that the barn plan is a good one because it will be the start of rehabilitating the whole area." said Mr Winfield. "The owner of the shops has often made this point." Mr Winfield said the problem for Mr McMonagle was to decide on the growth of his business in relation to a limited site. He said he was not unsympathetic to the fact there was a problem for Mr McMonagle, but it was in the nature of the site.

ALL THAT REMAINS

All that remains of Hooe Barton Farm is the Elizabethan Threshing Barn, the Archway that belonged to the Chapel of St. Lawrence, a gatepost, some walls and marks in the pavement.

The Barn is built on a cross plan using limestone rubble walls which are 1metre thick and taper slightly to the top from the inside. It is very likely that the limestone would be from one of the local Hooe quarries. The inner walls were lime plastered and painted white with limewash throughout but this has now largely fallen away. There are pigeon holes on the outside of the north gable and these do not run through into the interior.

Barley or corn would be cut by hand with a sickle or scythe. The cutter followed by labourers who collect up the fallen stalks and tie them into large bundles, called sheaves. Four sheaves are propped together to form a stook so the cut crop can dry over the next few days.

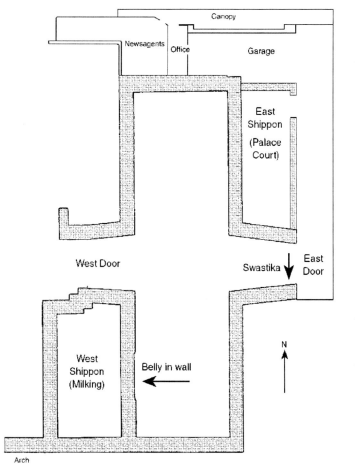

When dried off the sheaves were taken down to the threshing barn to have the grain separated from the straw. Corn or barley was grown much higher than todays version, about a metre high or more as a long straw length was useful for thatching and more convenient for handling. In the barn the corn was dropped onto the floor in the centre of the Barn and hit with flails, a short piece of wood attached to a handle with a stout leather strap. This beating dislodged the grains and the wind blew away the light chaff, which is the husk of the grain. The natural draft could be augmented by using a punkah type device consisting of a large canvas sheet suspended from a beam across the west door. This could be waved so causing a considerable draft. The straw was picked up and stacked then the grain shovelled into sacks. The cupboard that held the grease for the flail's leather hinge and the remains of the beam for the canvas sheet can still be seen. See photos overleaf.

When Wimpey replaced the half hipped roof in 1968 they replaced most of the original oak timbers with modern ones.

Shippons were constructed, also of limestone rubble, between the north gable wall and the east door (Palace Court) and between the south gable wall and the west door. These appear to be later additions that affected the roof line as blocked up windows can be seen on the inner walls opposite the shippon's roof. The corrugated iron shippon along the west wall from the north gable wall have been pulled down and the site is now an area of ornamental trees.

There are signs that there was another lightweight shippon on the south east wall and may have been a garden store or poultry shed.

The windows are unglazed slit windows that taper outwards towards the interior and were designed to provide light and ventilation whilst keeping out the worst of the weather.

The floor is mainly cobbled though covered with a layer of pigeon guano. Richard Tidmarsh states that it would have originally been covered with smooth oak planks when used as a threshing barn to aid winnowing and collecting the grain.

The west door is higher than the east. Explanations vary regarding the reason. One is that it would have the effect of increasing draft from the prevailing south westerly winds, another that a full cart of sheaves is higher than an empty one so it was not necessary to build two high doors.

The general state of repair is poor. Slates continually slip from the roof, one of the skylights has been without glass for at least ten years and the guttering is largely missing. Excuses for inaction, hollow interest and sympathy are legion. Actually doing something is non-existent. Small trees and plants grow from the walls, a crack in the south east corner remains unattended, slates are not replaced and PCC's own identified urgencies are not acted upon. Ignoring the more complex and expensive task of converting the barn for community use, basic inexpensive maintenance has appeared difficult for PCC.

As property and land has been developed around the Barn it has become landlocked. Two other landowners abut the barn on the south, west, north and part of the eastern sides, making future development less straightforward but not impossible.

Hooe Barton Farm and surrounding development 1999.
Photograph courtesy of Western Morning News/Evening Herald.

The arch of the Manor Chapel of St. Laurence.

An unexplained belly into the south west wall. It does not appear to be a worn feature.

The Grease Cupboard. Thought to be where the grease was kept for greasing the threshing flails.

Door catch on the chapel arch.

Looking north from the south wall.

The Barn from the south east and what was part of the farm garden.

North wall showing blocked up windows and door into Palace Court, (East Shippon).

Threshing machine bearer marks near north wall.

Swastika painstakingly carved into a stone by east door.

South wall from midway point.

Exterior. South gable end. Remains of living room fireplace.

West door. The stub end of round beam projecting from the upper south west wall is thought to be the remains of the beam that supported a canvas sheet that could be swung like a Punkah to make extra draft for winnowing while threshing.

Hooe Barn from the south west corner. The chimney belonged to the farmhouse kitchen fireplace that was built into the breast protruding from the barn wall.

The student's conversion and use suggestion of which most people approved. The Barn as a Media/Arts Centre. This would comprise of a ground floor that had meeting/exhibition space. A workshop/studio area in the east shippon (Palace Court) and a kitchen in the west shippon. A mezzanine floor with disabled access would be added across half the length to make an interpretation centre. A separate toilet block would be added outside to the east. Car parking on the land occupied by The Lake Stores which would be demolished. Design Copyright Plymouth University 2000.

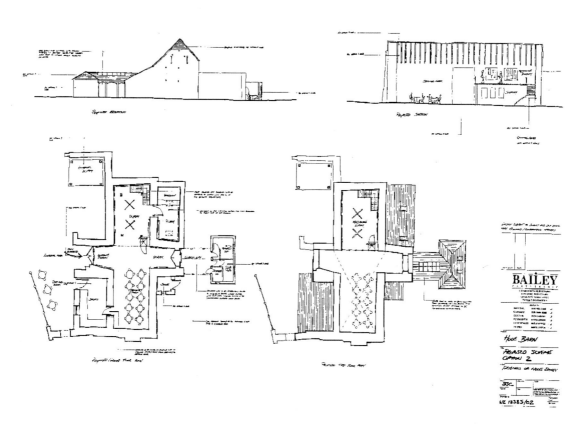

Bailey Partnership, as members of the 'ProHelp Group' looked at the student's ideas and drew up the above plan. It is feasible and would cost £258,000 for the development. The above drawing copyright Bailey Partnership, 2001.